PROPHET
AND WITNESS
IN JERUSALEM

PROPHET AND WITNESS IN JERUSALEM

A Study of the Teaching of Saint Luke

BY

ADRIAN HASTINGS

*Ecce, veniet propheta magnus, et ipse renovabit
Jerusalem, alleluja.*
ANTIPHON FROM THE FIRST SUNDAY OF ADVENT

HELICON PRESS, INC.

BALTIMORE MARYLAND

First Published 1958

Library of Congress Card Catalogue No. 58-13822

HELICON PRESS INC.
5305 EAST DRIVE,
BALTIMORE 27, MD.

MADE AND PRINTED IN GREAT BRITAIN BY WILLIAM
CLOWES AND SONS, LIMITED, LONDON AND BECCLES.
NIHIL OBSTAT ROLAND D. POTTER, O.P. IMPRIMATUR
+ J. KIWANUKA, BISHOP OF MASAKA, MASAKA, UGANDA.
11TH OCTOBER, 1957.

TO MGR FELICE CENCI

BEST OF RECTORS

AND TO MY BROTHERS OF THE URBAN COLLEGE

THE WORLD OVER

CONTENTS

PREFACE

THIS book is intended for all those who are seriously interested in the New Testament, and its aim is to investigate the particular character of one very important part of the latter: the third gospel and the Acts of the Apostles, the two books which we owe to St Luke.

Needless to say, this investigation is neither comprehensive nor final; nor is the treatment of all points equally detailed. I have concentrated on those parts where I feel I have something valuable to say of my own, either because they interest me more, or because they have been somewhat passed over in this country or by Catholic writers.

I owe much to the advice and help of friends both in Rome and in England: in Rome, to friends at Propaganda, firstly Monsignor Garofalo, then very many others who have assisted me in one way or another, among whom I would like to mention Father Bob Rose; in England, to Father Edmund Hill, O.P., who most kindly lent me a lively unpublished thesis entitled 'Messianic Fulfillment according to the Gospel of St Luke', to Mr and Mrs Sheed, and above all to my mother and members of the family, especially my sister Cecily, who at a difficult moment carried through a careful revision of the whole work. For the help of all, named and unnamed, many thanks.

I am proud to dedicate this, my first book, whose subject is the gospel of the Gentiles, to the members of my Roman college, where men of every race and continent live together in the dearest of fellowships.

ADRIAN HASTINGS

ACKNOWLEDGMENTS

SOME excerpts from Scripture have been translated by the author, others are from published translations. We are indebted to his Grace the Archbishop of Westminster, Messrs. Burns Oates & Washbourne Ltd., and Messrs. Sheed & Ward, Inc., for extracts from Mgr Ronald Knox's version of the Bible, Copyright 1944, 1948 and 1950, Sheed and Ward, Inc., New York.

AND I TOO, MOST NOBLE THEOPHILUS

HOLY Scripture is the written word of God, bearing witness to His living Word, Our Lord Jesus Christ. Here the Christian must come to learn of Christ, and here the Church interprets with authority because it is within the Church that the Christian finds scripture; it is a Church book. If the Church's authority interprets the Scriptures, it does not substitute for them; to gain personal knowledge of Our Lord Jesus Christ—and that is at the heart of our religion—scripture reading is of the utmost importance, indeed 'to be ignorant of the Scriptures is to be ignorant of Christ' as St Jerome long ago remarked and as Pope Pius XII has recently reaffirmed.[1] Today this truth is very adequately recognized, but the difficulty of understanding scripture remains as great as ever. An initial difficulty is the complexity of the New Testament; where the reader expects one book, he finds more than twenty. These are different works, written by different people of varying nationality, language and country, over a period of at least fifty years. Once this fact is grasped, priorities naturally appear, and three peaks come to stand out: first, the synoptics; then, St John; thirdly,

[1] Encyclical *Divino Afflante Spiritu*, 1943.

St Paul : the first because they seem nearest to Our Lord himself, the other two as the most powerful minds operating within the early Church. Among the synoptics the focal point is undoubtedly Mark, and after him Matthew. The third gospel, of St Luke, tends to fall between two stools : not so 'primitive' as Mark or Matthew, not so profound as John. In consequence, with the exception of the first two chapters and a few parables it is rather neglected. In recent years several books have been published in this country about St Mark, and many others about the theology of St John and St Paul, but there has been no comparable treatment of the doctrine of St Luke. This is a pity. St Luke's writings—the Third Gospel and the Acts— form the largest single coherent literary bloc within the New Testament; they provide a bridge between the earlier gospels and St John; and, as the work of a gentile and Greek-minded Christian, they have a character of their own.

Modern studies of St Luke have either concentrated on paragraph criticism, the examination of the exact literary relationship between his text and the earlier gospels, or they have treated of St Luke the man, doctor and travelling companion of St Paul, together with the cultural *milieu* of the Mediterranean world in which he lived. The scope of the present work is rather different. Its aim is to give a coherent view of St Luke's teaching as a whole, looked at theologically more than historically, and especially in so far as it is peculiar to himself. Within the common framework of early Christian doctrine, I am concerned with St Luke's particular approach and interests, the special themes to which he keeps returning, the conscious or unconscious preoccupations which made him stress one incident and pass over another. Unless one appreciates the special angle from which each of the gospel writers approached the life of Our Lord, one is bound to miss a large part of his message. The thought of the evangelists is much less simple, less easily appreciated, than one may imagine, for they were gifted men writing about the supreme mystery: inspired by the Spirit, heirs of a unique religious tradition, living in a world quite different from our own and using a literary idiom to which we are not accustomed.

Dr Dodd has remarked that 'it is a great merit of modern critical study of the New Testament that it has made us appreciate the individuality of the great theologians of the apostolic age, and the rich diversity of their teaching'.[1] This is of course particularly true of John and Paul, but it must be applied too to the synoptic writers; until we realize this, we shall never understand the gospels. It is not sufficient to admit that there is a 'synoptic teaching', no, there is a Matthaean, a Markan, and a Lucan teaching, and their finer points must inevitably be blurred if, instead of considering them in themselves, we interpret them in terms of their neighbours. Of course we have to go from one to the other, of course they are never contradictory and often mutually enlightening, but they remain distinct works meriting distinct consideration. The theology of the New Testament will be so much the richer when we see it as the vast synthesis of different theological patterns, first understood by themselves, and not simply as the aggregate of a mass of isolated texts indiscriminately selected.

It may be objected that St Luke was the least theologically minded of the New Testament writers, the 'pure historian', and therefore not a good subject for this sort of treatment. But it is a pity to minimize Luke's intellectual powers; the Lucan contribution to Christian thought is not exhausted by describing

[1] C. H. Dodd, *According to the Scriptures*, p. 13.

it as the gospel of mercy or the universal gospel. All the early Christians were theologians, Luke among them, and it is our business, not his, to unravel his theology; it is worth the effort. What we have to look for is sometimes a consciously formulated idea, sometimes a mental presupposition, a way of seeing things taken for granted by the writer and colouring his whole approach, but not always explicitly formulated or even perhaps fully conscious.

The relation of history to theology in gospel writing is a delicate question, only now receiving the serious attention it deserves. No solution of it may sacrifice one to the other: such a course would be a betrayal of both. Evangelical history is only told at all because it is theologically significant; evangelical theology is always theology of what has actually happened, is actually happening, or will certainly actually happen in the future. Luke's theology cannot falsify, but it does interpret history: in his work we see the true Jesus, but we see him through the mind of St Luke.

The early Christians—Luke was no different—were not simply interested in recording the words of Jesus, their work of recording was also a work of interpretation: the fitting of individual incidents and sayings within the whole revealed economy of divine salvation. No one writer then or now could adequately express this economy, and though his work was inspired it remained personal. Some writings are more intensely personal than others; thus one feels that St John managed to 'Joannize' all his material far more completely than St Luke managed to 'Lucanize' his; hence it is easier in the third gospel to penetrate through to the pre-Lucan material than in the fourth to penetrate through to the pre-Joannine.

That brings us to the very important point that St Luke was writing within a tradition; and his book only had value for the first Christians, and was only canonized by the Church, because it was far more than a personal work. It is an ecclesiastical, an orthodox book in which the author has been faithful to the teaching of authority, not a schismatic or heretical one in which the author would propound a private doctrine or revelation. If we are to understand St Luke's work, we have to see it in this way. From the Church and from fellow Christians who had been privileged to witness the events he speaks of, he obtained his factual information and also its basic interpretation.

Before the gospels there was the Gospel, that is to say the apostolic proclamation of good news about Jesus Christ, about God's decisive intervention in the life of the world. The gospels, as we know them, are written statements of this original Gospel, and their central purpose is the same. They *proclaim* Christ, are never mere biographies or works of history, nor of course essays in abstract theology. Rather do they state facts pregnant with theological meaning for a definite purpose—to produce or strengthen faith. This was the purpose of the original apostolic preaching and catechesis, and, when oral teaching and tradition were felt to be insufficient, of the written documents as well. The development was wholly natural. In a world where much was written and much read, Christians, even though belonging mostly to the less educated classes, quickly felt the need for written accounts of Jesus' life and work. Doubtless our gospels were not the first writings of this kind, but their predecessors may have been less complete. The surviving gospels drew on these others and soon replaced them. I am not concerned with the details of this process. Sufficient to say that

Matthew and Mark had written before Luke, and that while appreciating the value of their work he felt there was room for a further book. He had, as we shall see, his own approach to the life of Christ, and he wanted furthermore to link it with the subsequent growth of the Christian Church; seen in the light of Acts, in fact, Luke's work seems remarkably different from that of the first two synoptics. Again, he wanted something written in passable Greek, adapted in its all-round appearance to the sort of Christians or future Christians he knew in Philippi and Antioch.

The essential historicity of his account of the life of Christ and the origins of the Church is both critically well-guaranteed and absolutely required for the end he had in view. People in those days were as aware as we are of the difference between fact and myth, and Luke wrote of what he believed to be fact; he was indeed unusually concerned with factual precision, especially in his account of those events—such as the Resurrection appearances—which are now most easily labelled myths. He wrote of events which had taken place for the most part only thirty or forty years previously, events which many—both friends and enemies—could still remember without difficulty, public events in which famous public characters had played their part.

The central ideas of the third gospel were in no way special to St Luke. They belonged to common Christian teaching, which took the form of explaining the chief incidents of Our Lord's life in terms of the Old Testament, 'according to the Scriptures'. Without the Old Testament we cannot understand the New; and though it might be thought that that axiom applies far less to the third gospel than to the others, because its author—maybe alone—was a Gentile, someone born outside the Jewish tradition, in fact it applies quite as much. It is no exaggeration to say that this, if any, is the gospel of the fulfilment of scripture, of 'what has been fulfilled among us' (Lk. 1:1), from Jesus' opening words at Nazareth to his supreme conclusion 'All that was written of me in the law of Moses, and in the prophets, and in the psalms, must be fulfilled' (Lk. 24:44). In these last years there has been a growing appreciation of the profound inter-penetration of the two testaments; it is one of the most valuable aspects of modern biblical study. Throughout this book I shall try to indicate the Old Testament background to St Luke's thought, the framework into which he fitted the ideas of the new revelation, the texts according to which he interpreted the saving events of the Lord's life. Many of the texts had already entered common Christian doctrine, basic to apostolic preaching and catechesis. Christian teaching was pre-eminently a class in exegesis. Other texts used by Luke were more personal to him and relate more directly to the themes which are special to his own gospel. There is no question here of the mere fulfilment of isolated Old Testament prophecies, but of the weaving of the whole texture of the New Testament out of that of the Old.

There are parts of the New Testament—the earliest parts— which seem to belong in a very special way to the Old Testament tradition; the reason is the continuity of thought existing between the earliest Christian community and the Jewish *milieu* in which it was born. Our Lord's own teaching can be understood only within that *milieu*. Among these parts are the first chapters of the third gospel, and I cannot accept them as in origin Luke's own work for this very reason. They are written from within the old Jewish tradition, while his own use of the Old Testament has a rather different character. He knew the Old Testament excellently and used it unceasingly, but as someone culturally outside, not fully at home in the Jewish mental world of the last years preceding Christ; and he wrote for people with the same background as himself. What was substantially the same exegesis required a different form of presentation, and had to make use of somewhat different images and explanatory ideas. Consequently St Luke's own Old Testament exegesis stands already a little removed from the earliest Christian form, found best in Mark. Luke's is moving in the direction of later patristic exegesis, although his fidelity to the materials he had gathered together and his closeness to the gospel events make his work at the same time an invaluable vehicle for some very early Christian thought. It is impossible to distinguish precisely his personal contribution from the traditional doctrine which he received and was trying to illustrate, but without applying this distinction where possible one cannot appreciate Luke's own contribution to Christian theology or the peculiar character and value of the third gospel.

If in writing his gospel Luke was controlled on the one hand by the common teaching of the Church, on the other he was dependent for detailed information on particular sources. As a convert from Antioch, personally unacquainted with the Lord, his information had all to be at least second-hand. He was controlled by his sources; and the great majority of things which Jesus said or did he can never have heard about at all, any more than we have heard of them. But there is no reason whatsoever to believe that he merely collected a lot of traditions and tied them together with a series of 'ands' and 'buts'; his book has unity of style and thought and asserts itself as the work of one author. Evidently he did not write all he had heard, and if his sources controlled him, he also controlled them, selecting and adapting to his own purposes. There are those nowadays who want to make everything in the gospels derive from the corporate tradition or religious imagination of one Church or another. Now doubtless the Churches had established traditions about the great events of the Lord's life, and that Luke and the other evangelists knew of these traditions and learnt from them one can easily admit. But when St Luke set about writing on the life of Jesus it is most unlikely that he would limit himself to a collection of such traditions. Why should he? There were lots of people about who had known Jesus personally, who had witnessed this event or that one. They were the obvious people to go to. Hence I do not apologize for speaking of John and Joanna and Simeon rather than of different types of folk tradition developing in such-and-such a community.

But we cannot always pin down sources like that, and the chief Christian communities must evidently have possessed and cherished communal memories; hence the traditions of Jerusalem and Antioch can indeed be the source of much in the gospels, and I think furthermore that the third gospel had a definite local colour, that of its author's home, Antioch. Antioch was the mother of gentile Christianity, the starting point for Paul's journeys. Our gospel has the broad interests of this church; a deep Old Testament foundation on the one hand, freedom from Judaist scrupulosity on the other. It is the universal, the Greek, the gentile gospel.

Sources and the author's *milieu* cannot be ignored then; they are, after all, the cords binding the book to its subject, and their character explains much about its shape and themes. That is why the first chapters of this work are concerned with sources, and only afterwards do I tackle Luke's own theology as an intelligible whole which makes use of, but is not simply identifiable with, the ideas of his informants. What is important is to avoid the sort of *either/or* which is too common in modern scholarship. Either everything is explained in terms of its sources, or of its dogmatic preoccupations. But this type of dilemma is unnecessary. History and theology are not irreconcilable. It is more sensible to suppose that the gospels derive their character both from their source material and from the minds of their authors, and contain both history and interpretation—even extensive theological symbolism.

Certainly I am more concerned with Luke as a Christian thinker than as a historian, with the interpretation rather than with the narration of fact; also less with common doctrine than with what was personal to St Luke. We cannot separate the two, forming as they do only one living texture of thought, but I do pass rapidly over the great dominical teachings—Jesus' own theology. This centred round the revelation of the Father, of the kingdom, of the last times; and of his own person as revealer of the Father, inaugurator of the kingdom, and central character in the last times begun already with his appearance on earth and to be terminated by his triumphal return. This personal teaching Jesus expressed in terms of the 'Son of Man' of Daniel, the 'Servant of the Lord' of Isaias, and the messianic king of psalm 109.[1] These are the fundamental themes of Jesus' teaching, out of which, with the help of the powerful illumination of passion and resurrection, the vast structure of Christian theology has legitimately developed. But I consider them here in their specifically Lucan context and in so far as St Luke gave them a new emphasis.

[1] References to the psalms follow the Vulgate numbering throughout.

There are certainly dangers in the new theological approach to the gospels, for example, that of explaining away history as symbolism. Such-and-such a thing never happened but the writer puts it in to illustrate some higher truth. This is nonsense. We are throwing out the baby with the bath water, the essence of the true gospel message with the historical style of a later day which we now know is not to be found in the gospels. Symbolism is there indeed, but symbolism rooted in real events; symbolism implanted not just by man, but by God. If it is the writer's own, it is based on fact; he manifests the significance of words and events by rearranging and adapting, but not inventing or falsifying, the facts of the case. Another danger is to discover too much theology, to read meanings into things which the evangelists never intended. This is also a very real danger, and one which is not altogether being avoided at present. Its worst effect is bound to be the discredit of theological interpretation on account of its excessive or subjective use. I feel, for instance, that the attempt to divide up the third gospel according to the books of Moses and see St Luke's work as a Christian hexateuch is unjustifiable as a forced and artificial comparison, and at the same time gravely obscures the true divisions and thought structure of the book in favour of an *a priori* arrangement which has in fact very little to recommend it. On the other hand, if we deny that St Luke was a theologian in favour of the 'pure historian' how shall we ever explain his inversion of the Matthaean temptation order or his silence on the post-Resurrection appearances in Galilee?

A word about St Luke's fondness for duality. It is found all through the structure of his writing, pre-eminently in the relation of Gospel and Acts—two parts of a single whole. They are united by a multitude of common themes, by their internal parallelism and continuity of plot: from Jesus to the Church, but the Spirit in both. The parallel openings are important; in each case the descent of the Spirit, on Jesus in the Jordan, on the disciples at Pentecost; each is followed by an inaugural address, based on an Old Testament text. Jesus gives his at Nazareth and uses a passage from Isaias, Peter at Jerusalem and bases himself on Joel. There are several other examples of dual structure, and in each case the first part is preparatory for the second, in which it finds its achievement. Thus there is the parallelism between the birth of John and that of Jesus; and there is the Galilean ministry, followed by the journey to Jerusalem. In the Acts there is the section centring on Peter and the section centring on Paul. An awareness of this device is useful for understanding more important matters and relating individual parts to the complete literary scheme.

Finally, a word about St Luke himself. The 'Anti-Marcionite prologue', a preface to the gospel written before the end of the second century, says that 'Luke was a Syrian of Antioch, physician by profession, who became a disciple of the Apostles and later accompanied Paul until his martyrdom. Serving the Lord steadfastly, unmarried and childless, he died at the age of 84 in Boetia, full of the Holy Spirit'.[1] Coming from the cradle

---

[1] Luke's Antiocene origin is mentioned by Eusebius and Jerome and seems generally probable. It is also supported by a reading in the 'Western' text of Acts (Codex Bezae and others). The longer readings of this Western text are normally regarded as interpolations, but their origin is at least very ancient. This one, in chapter 11:28, speaks of the early days of the Church of Antioch. The additional words of the Western text are in italics: 'At this time, some prophets from Jerusalem visited Antioch, *and there was great joy. When we were gathered together,* one of these, Agabus by name, stood up and prophesied.' As an interpolation, this would seem very pointless. As a genuine Lucan addition, it would indicate, most unobtrusively, the author's Antiocene origin and trustworthiness as a chronicler.

of gentile Christianity, it is not surprising that St Luke should have been especially attracted by St Paul, the apostle of the Gentiles. When they first met we do not know, but the evidence of the Acts shows us that Luke accompanied the Apostle on more than one of his missions. The evidence lies in those intriguing and fascinating sections of the Acts called the 'we' passages, sections of particularly detailed and well-informed narrative written in the first person plural.[1] The author of these passages, Luke, was with Paul on the second missionary journey when he crossed from Troas to Philippi, where presumably he remained, as we find him there on Paul's third mission. Then he accompanied the apostle via Troas, Miletus and Caesarea to Jerusalem. After Paul's imprisonment at Caesarea Luke was with him again, with Aristarchus the Macedonian, for the journey to Rome; and at Rome Acts comes to an end.

From the epistles we learn that Luke remained with Paul during his first Roman captivity. 'Greetings from my beloved Luke, the physician, and from Demas' (Col. 4:14). Again, 'Greetings to you from Epaphras, my fellow prisoner in Christ Jesus; from Mark, Aristarchus, Demas and Luke, who share my labours' (Philem. 23–24). Finally in 2 Timothy 4:10, written some time later, perhaps during a second Roman imprisonment, 'Crescens has gone to Galatia, Titus to Dalmatia, and Luke is my only companion.' And that is all we know about St Luke.[2]

[1] Acts 16:10–17; 20:5—21:25; 27:1—28:16.

[2] We should of course know more about St Luke than we do, if it were possible to follow Dr E. C. Selwyn who in *St Luke the Prophet* (Macmillan, 1901) charmingly identified him with Silas, Silvanus, and even the Tertius of Romans 16:22. This many-named and phenomenally active personality besides writing the third gospel and Acts, and committing Romans to paper, also

Few would now dispute either that the third gospel and the Acts were written by one man, or that that man was Luke. When he wrote is not so clear. Conceived as one work, the two books must have been written at about the same time. As the Acts end abruptly in Rome during Paul's first imprisonment there, it seems most reasonable to conclude that they were written at that time, A.D. 61–63. If they were written after Paul's martyrdom in Rome, it is astonishing that they make no mention of it, for Luke's story could have had no more apposite conclusion. But an argument from silence is never wholly conclusive, and one cannot quite rule out a rather later date. The much disputed issue is whether Luke wrote before or after the fall of Jerusalem in A.D. 70, and as this question may be thought of special importance for an understanding of Luke's whole work, I shall return to it at the close of the book.[1]

wrote both 1 and 2 Peter, with of course St Peter's full permission, in order to reconcile him with St Paul.

1 Appendix: 'The Holy City'.

2

MANY HAVE SET FORTH THE HISTORY
OF WHAT HAS BEEN FULFILLED AMONG US

IN this chapter I will briefly discuss the chief written sources of which St Luke most probably made use. The best place to start a study of his authorities is with his own preface and acknowledgements:

> Many have been at pains to set forth the history of what time has brought to fulfilment among us, following the tradition of those first eye-witnesses and ministers of the word.[1] And I too, most noble Theophilus, have resolved to put the story in writing for thee as it befell, having first traced it carefully from its beginnings, that thou mayst understand the instruction thou hast already received, in all its certainty. (Lk. 1:1–4.)

In writing this, Luke's aim is not strictly to make his acknowledgements or cite his authorities. It is rather a self-vindication. How dare he, Luke, set about writing the gospel story? He answers that it has been done already and by 'many', distinguishing these from a more exalted group of 'eye-witnesses and ministers of the word'. He is on a level with the many; what they have done, why should not he do? Like them

---

[1] I desert Mgr Knox's translation for this phrase. It runs 'of those first eye-witnesses who gave themselves up to the service of the word', and thus merges the two groups, which are, I think, to be distinguished.

he has learnt from the tradition of the eye-witnesses and accredited teachers, and will take care to write in order and with
accuracy. However, in making this little defence Luke does
reveal the sort of authorities of which he, who had no personal
direct knowledge of the Lord's life, had made use. Evidently
he had studied the accounts of the 'many'. He does not say
who they are, nor what their writings were like; probably
several of these were short enough, others, like St Mark's
gospel which he certainly knew, of greater length. It is generally thought that Luke could not have intended to include
St Matthew's gospel in this general reference, because that was
the gospel of an apostle, and he distinguishes the 'many' from
the 'eye-witnesses and ministers of the word'; as St Matthew
was most certainly one of the latter, it is argued, he could not
also be one of the former; but perhaps this is to read too much
into Luke's words. The difference was rather of function: St
Luke wishes to say that basing themselves on recognized
teaching some have written ordered accounts of the
gospel events of a more personal character. Furthermore
the first gospel, most probably read by Luke in one or
another of the Greek translations made somewhat haphazard,
as Papias tells us, from the Aramaic original, may hardly
have appeared to him as a strictly apostolic gospel at all.
Without title, it would have been simply the most important
account of the Lord's life current in Christian circles in his
time.

Luke's literary relations with Mark have been minutely
studied time and again, and I will only treat of them here in the
briefest possible way. Luke presumably read Mark's gospel for
the first time after arriving with Paul in Rome. He at once
recognized its value due to its vivid, dramatic character and the

weight of the Petrine authority behind it; and he decided to incorporate large parts of it, with only minor changes, in his own narrative. It is generally agreed that Luke depends on the second gospel for all those very considerable parts which they (and St Matthew) have in common. Thus, very generally, Luke 4:31—6:19 depends on Mark 1:21—3:19; Luke 8:4—9:50 on Mark 4:1—9:39; and Luke 18:15-43 on Mark 10:13-52. This dependence is not always equally close, and these passages may include some non-Marcan material. St Luke is always fairly free with stylistic changes, but at times, as in the Transfiguration story, he does more, either because he has obtained additional information or in order to bring out an idea of his own. Luke's debt to Mark was evidently very great; perhaps indeed too great, for one feels that he did not succeed in digesting his Marcan borrowings sufficiently and they stand as a result somewhat apart from the central themes of the third gospel. This immense use of Mark is best explained by Luke's undoubted reverence for St Peter, most authoritative witness of Jesus' ministry and Resurrection. If Marcan material bulks so large in the pages of the third gospel it is because it represented for Luke the testimony of Peter himself.

Turning from the 'triple tradition' (material common to Matthew, Mark and Luke) to the 'double tradition' (the sections common only to Matthew and Luke) we find that these passages are not located in two or three large blocks, like the former, but are scattered about up and down the third gospel. Good examples are Luke 12:39-46, to be compared with Matthew 24:43-51; and Luke 7:18-35, to be compared with Matthew 11:2-19 (but in the latter note the omission by Luke of verse 14). Again, these portions of Luke have received

2

intensive study; the problem of their relationship with the first gospel is an important one, but not one which I intend to examine at length. It is evident that either Luke here depends on Matthew, or Matthew on Luke, or both on a now lost third work. No one supposes that Matthew depends on Luke, hence either Luke used Matthew or—as most scholars hold—they both used a third source, which has been given the famous name of Q, and whose existence was until recently almost a dogma of scientific faith, but is now coming in for some severe questioning. M. Vaganay, a distinguished French Catholic scholar, has recently presented a rather complicated solution of his own,[1] cutting up the old Q into M and S, two Aramaic documents, of which M would be the original gospel of St Matthew, but very different from the later canonical version. St Luke, M. Vaganay thinks, did not know of our canonical Matthew, but did make use of a Greek translation of the earlier version. In two other recent studies Abbot Butler and Doctor Farrer accept Luke's dependence on canonical Matthew,[2] but subsequently to this Abbot Butler has admitted that the Matthew which Luke knew may indeed have been a kind of first edition somewhat different from the Matthew which we know today.[3] This seems to me both the simplest and most likely solution to the problem. It is difficult to understand how the careful and widely-travelled Luke could have missed the first gospel if it had appeared before he wrote; and it probably had, as St Paul seems to make use of it in the epistles

[1] L Vaganay, *Le Problème Synoptique.*

[2] B. C. Butler, *The Originality of St Matthew* (Cambridge, 1951); A. M. Farrer, 'On Dispensing with Q', in *Studies in the Gospels* (Blackwell, 1955), pp. 55–88.

[3] 'The Synoptic Problem Again', *Downside Review*, winter 1954/5, pp. 24–46.

to the Thessalonians[1]; if Paul knew Matthew it is almost inconceivable that Luke did not do so as well.

The parts of the third gospel which interest me most, however, are not those which Luke owed to Matthew and Mark, but those which are not paralleled elsewhere. These very considerable portions include chapters 1–2, most of the famous 'central section' 9:51—18:14, and a great deal of Luke's Passion and Resurrection narrative. It is above all the source for the central section which worries the critics; whence did Luke obtain his information about this whole part of Jesus' ministry on which the other evangelists are almost silent? about the mission of the Seventy-two? about such parables as those of the Good Samaritan, the Prodigal Son, and the Publican and the Pharisee? The great value of this section, and also its rather mysterious character, are widely recognized. Lagrange said that it was 'of priceless value', while Vaganay has called it 'the treasure of Luke'.[2] Some have thought that behind it there was another single document, called by the name of 'Proto-Luke', and perhaps actually written by Luke himself before writing the complete gospel (i.e. before merging it with the material drawn from the gospel of St Mark). But this theory of 'Proto-Luke' has really very little to be said in its favour and is now generally abandoned. The central section of Luke is a patchwork, based in part perhaps on short documents, but mostly on the oral tradition of those whom St Luke consulted; and this has permitted him to leave here the impress of his own mind more clearly than elsewhere; hence it is

[1] Dom Bernard Orchard, 'Thessalonians and the Synoptic Gospels', *Biblica*, 1938; E. Cotenet, 'La iie Epitre aux Thessaloniciens et l'Apocalypse synoptique', *Recherches de Science religieuse*, 1954.

[2] Lagrange, *The Gospel of Jesus Christ* (Burns Oates, 1911), vol. 1, p. 5; L. Vaganay, *Le Problème Synoptique*, p. 108.

especially in this part that the great Lucan gospel themes appear.

There is only one other important written source behind the third gospel: it is that responsible for the first two chapters. In this connection it is first worth noticing that a recent study[1] has tried to show that the chief source behind the whole third gospel—the gospel of the gentiles—was no other than the Judaeo-Christian community of Jerusalem and St James, its head. Moreover, it is held, the latter was not only Luke's principal source but also that of St Paul, who was as we know very closely connected with Luke. It is true that Paul had been in close contact with James on various occasions, but it is equally clear that their approaches to Christian problems were strikingly diverse. Certainly it is not unlikely that Paul learnt a part of what he knew about the details of the Lord's life in the course of his various visits to Jerusalem and to James. Luke, during his long stay in Palestine before the journey to Rome, may also have learnt from the same source, though as a gentile Christian he would probably not have felt very comfortable in the atmosphere of the Church of Jerusalem. Behind some of Paul's and Luke's factual knowledge of Jesus' life it is permissible to see then the witness of James and the traditions of Jerusalem. However, the chief explanation of that immense concern with Jerusalem which has been noted as so striking a characteristic of the third gospel[2] lies not in Luke's sources so much as in his theology, in the plan and purpose of his gospel. This is particularly clear as a great many of his references to

[1] J. Staudinger, 'Testis primarius Evangelii sec. Lucam', *Verbum Domini* (1955), pp. 65–77, 128–42; see also J. Schmitt, 'Le Récit de la Résurrection dans l'Evangile de Luc', *Revue des Sciences Religieuses* (1951), pp. 119–37, 219–42.

[2] Staudinger, op. cit., p. 71.

Jerusalem have an obviously artificial character; they will be explained later, not by sources but by 'plot'.

To consider St Luke's as simply the gospel of the Church of Jerusalem, in contrast with the 'Galilean' gospels of Matthew and Mark, is to over-simplify. Galilee and Jerusalem were not the only places from which a gospel story could come, and were not all the churches daughters of Jerusalem? The tone of many of St Luke's references to Jerusalem is not at all what we should expect from the Judaeo-Christian Church there itself. More likely his debt was in the first place to his own Church of Antioch and its elders; Antioch was founded from Jerusalem, and doubtless its traditions incorporated some of those of the mother church. In so far as the third gospel can be said to be the gospel of any one Church, it is Antioch rather than Jerusalem, though probably St Luke actually wrote in Rome.

Nevertheless in the first two chapters of the third gospel we can fairly safely detect the immediate influence of the Christian community of Jerusalem, and so perhaps of James himself. These chapters form a literary unit in themselves and contrast sharply with most of the rest of the gospel on account of their strongly Judaic and Old Testament character; their theology, spirituality and language are all reminiscent of the old rather than the new dispensation. The stylistic difference between Luke's refined and very Greek preface ($1:1-4$) and the subsequent verses is most striking. These two chapters are at present undergoing intensive study. In a series of articles Dr Winter has produced convincing evidence to show that they were not in origin Luke's work, but the translation of a Hebrew original: their Old Testament references are closer to the Hebrew than they are to the Septuagint, and their etymological name references make no sense in Greek.[1] The theory, popularized by Harnack and still somewhat in vogue, that Luke was carefully shamming a septuagintal style in these chapters simply does not stand up to careful examination. Incidentally this conclusion gives strong support to the defence of the narrative's historical character; for if Harnack, and so many others, have tried to maintain that Luke had no written source, but wrote in a sham Old Testament style, it is largely because it is so much easier to deny historical value to a comparatively late Greek work of Luke than to an earlier account in Hebrew. Above all this has an important bearing on the historicity of the Virgin Birth which many[2] have tried to explain away as a

[1] Paul Winter, 'Some Observations on the language in the Birth and Infancy Stories of the Third Gospel', *New Testament Studies*, vol. 1, no. 2 (Nov. 1954), pp. 111–21; 'The Proto-Source of Luke I', *Novum Testamentum* (Leiden), vol. 1 (July 1956), pp. 184–99; and other studies. See also R. Laurentin, 'Traces d'allusions étymologiques en Luc 1–2', *Biblica*, 1956, pp. 435–56, and 1957, pp. 1–23. Dr Winter has rendered a real service in throwing light on the literary character and original language of Luke 1–2. Unfortunately, he wishes to explain away, and in the most arbitrary way, its historical value. The key point of his thesis is to deny the originally Christian character of Luke 1, which was written, he thinks, by disciples of John the Baptist as a mythical glorification of him in language borrowed from the epic of Samson. Luke 2 would be a Christian document imitating Luke 1 and modelling Our Lord's birth on that of John. How arbitrary all this is, is shown very effectively by P. Pierre Benoit, O.P., 'L'Enfance de Jean-Baptiste selon Luc I', *New Testament Studies*, 1957, pp. 169–94. P. Benoit clearly demonstrates the unity and integrally Christian character of Luke 1–2; he also, less successfully, maintains its Greek and Lucan literary origin. The latest complete study of the subject is René Laurentin's important book *Structure et Théologie de Luc I-II* (Gabalda, 1957). Unfortunately this did not come to hand until the present work was already in print. See also J. Coppens, 'L'Evangile lucanien de l'enfance', *Ephemerides Theologicae Lovanienses*, Oct.–Dec. 1957, pp. 729–35.

[2] For example, C. K. Barrett, *The Holy Spirit and the Gospel Tradition* (S.P.C.K., 1954), pp. 23–4.

Christian borrowing from Hellenic religion. In fact we find it in the most primitive and most Judaic parts of the New Testament (Lk. 1–2, Mt. 1) and hence those least likely to be influenced by the Greek world. Furthermore Luke's two chapters, dependent as they are on the Hebrew and not on the Septuagint, derive not only from a Jewish source, but from Palestinian, not Hellenistic, Judaism. The account of the Virgin Birth is an integral part of these two chapters, and hence cannot be explained away as a borrowing from some far-fetched 'parallel' discovered in a wholly different cultural *milieu*.

We have here, then, a document translated into Greek and adapted by Luke, but still preserving most of its original character, and full of fascinating detail which localizes the story so well in the Jewish world of that time: 'There was a priest called Zachary, of Abia's turn of office, who had married a wife of Aaron's family, by name Elizabeth' and so on (1:5). We don't know who the author was: certainly a member of the Christian-Jewish community of Palestine and probably of the Church of Jerusalem, ruled over by James. The sources of the story could have been many: James himself, of course, and other members of Jesus' family, but especially Our Lady. 'But Mary treasured up all these sayings, and reflected on them in her heart' (2:19) and again it is written that 'his mother kept in her heart the memory of all this' (2:51). What are these but gentle acknowledgements to the memory of a principal person in the story? And so it is not fanciful to call these chapters 'Our Lady's gospel'.

The aim of this little and wholly charming work was perhaps to convince the Jewish world that the best representatives of the true Israel had received Jesus in a most fitting way, and that there is no possible contradiction between the new and the old.

Zachary and Elizabeth, Joseph and Mary, Simeon and Anna, were all beautiful examples of Old Testament piety and devotion, and at the same time typified every side of Israel's life: priest, prophet and layman, the learned and the simple; yet they had all welcomed the messiah Jesus, and the Jewish Christians of the community of Jerusalem were only following their example. Just as John's birth reminds us of those of Isaac (Gen. 21) and Samson (Jud. 13), so Jesus' nativity is described in a traditional style which finds a model in the birth narrative of the prophet Samuel (1 Sam. 1–3).[1] The *Magnificat* is not unlike the canticle of Samuel's mother Anna, and as Samuel's birth was the answer to Anna's prayer so was Jesus' the answer to the prayer of all Israel. The narrative constantly takes us to the Temple, the centre of all religious life for the Jews, and further proof that Jesus is the expected Messiah is given in the stress on the Holy Spirit's presence. According to the prophets the Messiah and messianic times were to be full of the Spirit; our document shows this as fulfilled; and not only Jesus but all those near him are manifestly overflowing with the Spirit of God. What could this mean to a pious Jew except that the messianic era had begun?

This document may originally have been longer than the two first chapters of our gospel, including, for instance, such other matter as Our Lord's genealogy (3:23–38). It has often been remarked how similar in character the first chapters of the third gospel are to those of the Acts. This can easily be explained. The first part of the Acts vividly describes the atmosphere in the primitive Christian Church of Jerusalem, while it was in

---

[1] E. Burrows, S.J., in *The Gospel of the Infancy* (Burns Oates, 1940), pp. 1–51, studies the systematic parallelism which links Luke 1–2 with 1 Samuel 1–3.

just that atmosphere that the early chapters of the gospel were written; they naturally reflect the mentality of those who wrote them.[1] St Luke felt the special importance of this document and included it, translated into Greek but not much altered, in the book he was writing. It is highly probable that he knew St Matthew's account of Jesus' birth, but he easily realized that to incorporate matter from it would spoil the distinctive character of his own account, for the two were very different in scope. Once we rid our minds of the wholly false idea that the gospels were intended as mere chronicles of all the known facts, the difficulty about why St Luke ignores St Matthew's account of the infancy ceases to exist.

If Luke was not the primary author of his first two chapters, this does not mean that they do not fit into the higher plan of the third gospel. Though at first sight their tendency may seem very different from his own, yet I believe that he incorporated them quite deliberately, and that they fulfil a role of some importance within the complete thought-pattern of his writings.

[1] Luke 1–2 should be compared especially with Acts, 2:41—5:40 which M. Cerfaux considers ('La Première Partie du Livre des Actes', *Ephemerides Theologicae Lovanienses*, 1936, pp. 673–80) derive from a document characteristic of the church of Jerusalem. 'This document', he says, 'is remarkable for the religious and liturgical halo which surrounds it. The community hardly leaves the temple and all the incidents take the apostles back there again. The horizon is that of a bigoted Judaism, without any allusion to a world mission' (p. 679). This is rather strong, yet it can hardly be doubted that the community of Jerusalem was becoming ever further removed from the rest of the Church in its work and interests. It was Judaistic all the time, and tended to grow bigoted.

┌─────────┐
│   3   │
└─────────┘

THOSE FIRST EYE-WITNESSES AND
MINISTERS OF THE WORD

BEHIND even the earliest of Christian writings lay the tradition
of the first eye-witnesses and ministers of the word, and it was
on their memory and teaching that St Luke had finally to rely
for his knowledge of Our Lord's life. Unlike John and
Matthew, he could not write a gospel whose central thread was
personal reminiscence; unlike Mark, he was not the secretary
of any one apostle. In many ways Luke's has the character of a
last gospel; he is a second-generation writer, in close touch
with first-hand authorities but standing somewhat apart; his
account is consequently less vivid but traces better than the
others the general scheme of events. Though a 'follower and
disciple of the apostle', as St Irenaeus called him,[1] his gospel is
the least clearly *apostolic*, in that it gives less than the others the
direct witness of the apostles, and draws more on non-apostolic
sources of information. For all his personal initiative and original view-point Luke remains essentially dependent on his
sources—on the eye-witnesses and ministers of the word whom
he mentions in his gospel preface; who were they?

The word Luke uses here for eye-witness (αὐτόπτης) does
not appear elsewhere in the New Testament. But the complex

---

[1] *Cont. Haer.*, III, 10, 1.

and developing idea of a witness (μάρτυς) is one of essential
importance for early Christian thought, as also for the personal
theology of St Luke, and it will provide one of the themes of
this book. When Jesus was condemned by the Sanhedrin it was
for claiming to be the Messiah, the Son of Man, the Son of
God, with all that these titles implied. He was condemned for
blasphemy, after false witnesses had given testimony against him.
When he rose from the dead, he proved that the sentence had
been unjust and his claim true: he was the Messiah, Lord and
Son of God. The proof lay in his Resurrection, and so when the
apostles began preaching to their fellow Jews they witnessed
to the risen Jesus, they were the true witnesses producing the
essential evidence to substantiate Jesus' claim and prove his
judges wrong. They were enabled to do this by the power
of the Spirit: 'You will receive the power of the Spirit and you
will be my witnesses', Jesus had told them (Acts 1:8). To
the Jews of Jerusalem there was no need to preach on Our
Lord's life—they knew about it already. One only had to bear
witness to the fact of the Resurrection. So Peter said to the
twelve, 'There are men who have walked in our company all
through the time when the Lord Jesus came and went among
us, from the time when John used to baptize to the day when
he, Jesus, was taken from us. One of these ought to be added
to our number as a witness of his Resurrection' (Acts 1:21-2).
And again it is said, 'Great was the power with which the
apostles testified to the Resurrection of our Lord Jesus Christ'
(4:33). However, Christian preaching clearly did not for long
limit itself to the Resurrection alone; it naturally tended to
cover ever more of Jesus' life and preaching, and so the witness
came to be extended to all. The Christian witnessed to Jesus'
life 'from the time when John used to baptize to the day when

he, Jesus, was taken from us'. But it was personal witness given
by men who had been eye-witnesses, and these men were pre-
eminently the apostles. When Peter looks for someone to take
Judas' place, he looks for someone who can witness, who not
only believed in Jesus but had personal knowledge of his life.
So we arrive at a more fully developed idea of Christian witness,
given for instance by St Peter when speaking to the centurion
Cornelius. 'We are witnesses of all he [Jesus] did in the country
of the Jews, and in Jerusalem. And they killed him, hanging
him on a gibbet; but on the third day God raised him up again,
and granted the clear sight of him, not to the people at large,
but to us, the witnesses whom God had appointed beforehand;
we ate and drank in his company after his rising from the dead.
And he gave us a commission to preach to the people, and to
bear witness that he, and none other, has been chosen by God
to judge the living and the dead' (Acts 10:39–42).

At first the Christian witness (μαρτύριον) was rather different from the preaching (κήρυγμα): the former meant testifying
to the Jews of Jerusalem as to the fact of the Resurrection;
the latter included the publication of the whole Jewish-
Christian message of salvation to the world beyond the city.
The former was especially the work of the apostles, the latter
of every accredited Christian minister. However, these dis-
tinctions fairly rapidly blurred; by the time St Luke himself
wrote witness and *kerygma* had come to have much the same
meaning.[1]

The word 'witness' (μάρτυς) implied not only first-hand
knowledge but also a theological and ecclesiastical position.

[1] For a careful discussion of the idea of witness in the New Testament see
the studies of L. Cerfaux, 'Témoins du Christ', *Angelicum*, XX (1943), pp.
166–83; and A. Retif, 'Témoignage et Prédication Missionnaire dans les Actes
des Apôtres', *Nouvelle Revue Théologique*, 1951, pp. 152–65.

A 'witness' was one of 'those whom God had appointed beforehand', pre-eminently an apostle. But St Luke's appeal in his preface is simply to the *de facto* eye-witnesses (αὐτόπται) and while these certainly included the apostles, they were not limited to them; they could even include those who did not come at all into the second category of 'ministers of the word'.

This expression too had a somewhat general sense; Luke seems to mean the accredited preachers of the gospel message, men on whose word one could rely; doubtless they were largely the same as the first group of eye-witnesses, and for both groups the most notable members were the apostles; it was the memory of the apostles, the truly authoritative witnesses, which controlled the whole development of the gospel tradition and ensured that the special preoccupations of individual teachers did not cause perversions but only enrichments of the original message. The 'ministers of the word' implied a far larger group than the Twelve. The word used here for minister does not, it is true, appear often in the New Testament,[1] but St Paul speaks of the 'ministers of Christ' in 1 Corinthians 4:1 and in the context the title would seem to refer at least to himself, Cephas and Apollo. John Mark is called a minister in Acts 13:5 but he is evidently one of an inferior kind, a minister of Paul and Barnabas rather than of Christ. Only Paul is clearly given the title of minister, in Acts 26:16, in a phrase somewhat reminiscent of the Gospel preface: 'To this end have I appeared to thee, that I may make thee a minister and a witness of those things which thou hast seen and of those things wherein I will appear to thee.' Paul then was a minister and a witness, and so, strangely enough, it is he who

---

[1] ὑπηρέτης. The New Testament word most often translated by 'minister' is of course διάκονος.

seems to be most clearly referred to in the preface; but the point should not be pressed, especially as Paul was much more a witness than an eye-witness. Anyway 'minister' would seem to be a fairly general title; probably the evangelists, shepherds and doctors of Ephesians 4:11 could all be included in it, besides the apostles and prophets.

We do not know where the majority of the apostles were at the time that St Luke was collecting material for his gospel, but it is very probable that he was unable to consult them. However, among them, there were three who stood out as privileged with special knowledge and authority; they were Peter, James and John. If there were many events in Jesus' life which all the Twelve, but only they, had witnessed, there were others, such as the Transfiguration and the Agony in the garden, of which only this privileged inner group had first-hand knowledge. Luke may have spoken with all three, but most of what he owed to Peter he received through Mark, while James' contribution may be seen in the Jerusalem document. Luke's relations with John present us with a puzzle not easy to be solved. The somewhat 'Joannine' character of parts of the third gospel, such as its references to Satan, is coming to be more and more recognized. There are numerous resemblances between Luke's and John's accounts of the Passion and Resurrection; again John is a very likely source of Luke's special knowledge of the Transfiguration, which John himself does not speak of explicitly in his gospel. Luke's statement that the apostles 'saw his glory' (9:32) reminds us at once of the prologue of St John and its words 'we saw his glory' (Jn. 1:14). What was a single event for St Luke has apparently become a characteristic of Jesus' whole life for St John. Again, there is a close connection in the Resurrection accounts between Luke 24:12 and John

20:3–10. As it is not disputed that John wrote long after Luke, the general question is whether Luke was a literary source for John, or whether the similarities can be better explained—as I believe they can—by supposing that John was a factual and theological source for Luke.[1] Whatever the explanation, Luke appears as a sort of half-way house between Matthew and Mark on the one side and John on the other, and many typically 'Joannine' themes are already making their appearance in the third gospel. John was one of the most obvious people for Luke to approach for information and advice, as he was not only in Luke's eyes the most important of the Twelve apart from St Peter,[2] but he was also in a very special way a witness of the gospel events: 'He who saw it has borne his witness; and his witness is worthy of trust.'[3]

If part of Luke's material is Joannine, another part is doubt-less Pauline. Tradition makes Luke the interpreter of Paul, and this only confirms the evidence of the Acts and St Paul's epistles. We know that Luke was in Paul's company much of the time that he was preparing and writing his gospel, and his account of the Eucharistic institution[4] is very close to the

---

[1] The relations between the third and fourth gospels are studied precisely, but not very conclusively, by Canon Osty in 'Les Points de Contact entre le Récit de la Passion dans Saint Luc et Saint Jean', *Recherches de Science Religieuse*, 1951, 2–4 (*Mélanges Jules Lebreton*, I), pp. 146–54; and, by J. Schmitt, 'Le Récit de la Résurrection dans l'Evangile de Luc', *Revue des Sciences Religieuses*, 1951, pp. 119–37, 219–42.

[2] Cf. Acts 3:1–11; 4:7–22; 8:14.

[3] Jn. 19:35; see also Jn. 21:24; 1 Jn. 1:2; 4:14, etc.; Apoc. 1:2.

[4] Lk. 22:19–20. The absence of Luke 22:19b and 20 from the Western text has indeed made many critics judge them a mere later interpolation derived from Paul's parallel text. Though this is not impossible, it is equally far from proved, and raises far graver difficulties—I feel—than the acceptance of their authenticity.

Apostle's description of the same event in 1 Corinthians 11:24–5 and notably different from the Last Supper accounts of Matthew and Mark. Luke's general approach to Christianity with his stress on mercy and universality is, of course, akin to the Pauline view; but this means that he learnt his theology rather than his facts from St Paul. When we consider individual pieces of Gospel information, it does not help to name Paul as Luke's source as we have at once to ask who was Paul's source; it seems improbable that Paul had lesser details of the Lord's life directly revealed to him; more likely he too had to learn from others: from James, from St Matthew's gospel, but above all from the communities of Damascus, Jerusalem, Tarsus and Antioch, in which he moved during his first years as a Christian.

While Paul was in prison at Caesarea Luke had plenty of time to get to know that interesting character Philip the Evangelist, one of the seven original deacons and the father of four prophetesses. He lived in Caesarea, and Luke had already made his acquaintance when going up to Jerusalem in Paul's company (Acts 21:8–9). If anyone deserved the title of a 'minister of the word' it would be an evangelist, especially such an evangelist as Philip is shown to be in Acts 8. The very graphic account of Philip's activities there given was doubtless obtained from the man himself, and it was probably not the only information Luke gained from him. We do not exactly know what the functions of an evangelist were, the title only appearing three times in the New Testament. Apart from the reference to Philip (Acts 21:8), there is a bare mention among the list of offices in Ephesians 4:11, and there is St Paul's injunction to Timothy in 2 Timothy 4:5 to 'do the work of an evangelist'. Maybe it was simply a title given to one noted for his evangelical preaching work. Philip evangelized Jesus to the Ethiopian eunuch and afterwards continued the good work all the way to Caesarea (Acts 8:35 and 40) where he apparently settled down with his family. In Christian tradition 'evangelist' suggests not only missionary work but also specialized knowledge of the Lord's life, working on and interpreting a written gospel. This was the idea that Eusebius had of evangelists, and he gives us an example in Pantaenus, generally regarded as Clement's master in the early third-century school of Alexandria. He seems to have been a wandering teacher and exegete, perhaps hailing from Alexandria.[1] However it is quite a long way from Philip to Pantaenus, and we can hardly explain the office of the first by our very obscure knowledge of the life of the second. Anyway, Philip had been in Samaria, and Luke may owe to him at least his Samaritan information (Lk. 9:52-6; 17:11-19). For the rest he was, like Luke himself, not an eye-witness but a second-hand source; he was a deacon not an apostle.

After Philip I wish to say something, perhaps surprisingly, of Simon of Cyrene. What better source could Luke have had for his Passion narrative? Simon did not disappear from sight after the events of that day in which he had performed, perhaps reluctantly, a task which every Christian must for ever envy him. He remained well known in the Christian community—'Simon of Cyrene, the father of Alexander and Rufus' (Mk. 15:21). After the Resurrection and Ascension he may even have been one of the 'hundred and twenty' who remained

---

[1] Eusebius writes about evangelists in general in book III, chap. 27, of the *Ecclesiastical History*; while he speaks of Pantaenus in book V, chap. 10. For the latter see also Erik Peterson's notice 'Panteno' in the *Enciclopedia Cattolica*, IX, c. 693-4.

with the apostles and received the gift of the Spirit on the feast of Pentecost (Acts 1:15; 2:1). He was not the only Cyrenean in Jerusalem by any means—the Cyreneans even had a synagogue of their own—and there were men from Cyrene who heard the apostles speaking in their own tongue on that day of Pentecost (Acts 2:10). Among those converted one might number Lucius of Cyrene, perhaps a friend of Simon's. These too will have continued living with the Christian fellowship of Jerusalem, sharing in the prayer, the breaking of bread, the common life. Then came the episode of Stephen's preaching and martyrdom; the disciples dispersed and Simon and Lucius had to leave Jerusalem with the others (Acts 8:1). Where did they go? To Antioch.

> Meanwhile, those who had been dispersed owing to the persecution that was raised over Stephen had travelled as far away as Phoenice and Cyprus and Antioch, without preaching the word to anyone except the Jews. But there were some of them, men of Cyprus and Cyrene, who, when they found their way to Antioch, spoke to the Greeks as well, preaching the Lord Jesus to them. And the Lord's power went with them, so that a great number learned to believe, and turned to the Lord (Acts 11:19–21).

Of course we do not know that one of these Cyreneans was Simon, but when in 13:1 we read that 'the Church of Antioch had as its prophets and teachers Barnabas, and Simeon who was called Niger, and Lucius of Cyrene, and Manahen, foster-brother of Herod the tetrarch, and Saul', we may legitimately guess that Simeon the Black was Simon of Cyrene, called 'black' because of a skin darkened by the hot African sun of Cyrenaica and perhaps by a dose of negro blood as well.[1] Was

---

[1] It was Father Charles Runge who first suggested to me the identity of Simon of Cyrene and Simeon the Black.

his dark skin the reason why he was singled out to suffer the indignity of bearing a criminal's cross?

Simon's children, Alexander and Rufus, would seem to have gone later to Rome with their mother; it is why their names are mentioned in St Mark, the Roman gospel. Rufus was there when St Paul wrote the epistle to the Romans: 'My greetings to Rufus, a chosen servant of the Lord, and his mother, who has been a mother to me' (Rom. 16:13). When did St Paul get to know Rufus, and where did Rufus' mother have the chance to mother St Paul? Very probably during the year that Paul passed at Antioch among the prophets and teachers; Simon or Simeon and his wife were among the older members of the Christian community there, while Paul was still a young, unmarried preacher, on this supposition made welcome in Simon's household (Acts 11:26; 13:1).

It is most probable, as we know, that Luke came himself from Antioch. Evidently he knew the elders of the Church there well, and obtained what information they could give, especially about the origins of their own Antiocene Church. The Passion of St Stephen (chapters 6 and 7 of Acts) most probably belongs to a document which Luke incorporated in his own narrative; it describes the events which caused the first Christian exodus from Jerusalem and the consequent founding of the Church of Antioch. Its attitude towards Judaism and the temple is not that of the community of Jerusalem, but is more consonant with that of Antioch, where it probably originated. The reference to the synagogue of the Cyreneans (6:9) together with our knowledge that it was Cyreneans from Jerusalem who first preached to the gentiles of Antioch and then occupied an important place in that Church, suggest that this account was written by a Cyrenean, possibly Simon or Lucius.

The mission of Barnabas and Saul to Cyprus and Pisidia left Simeon the Black first on the list of Antioch's teachers, an important position. On their return,

> they called the Church together, and told the story of all God had done to aid them, and how, through faith, he had left a door open for the Gentiles. And they stayed there a considerable time with the disciples. But now some visitors came down from Judaea, who began to tell the brethren, You cannot be saved without being circumcised according to the tradition of Moses. Paul and Barnabas were drawn into a great controversy with them; and it was decided that Paul and Barnabas and certain of the rest should go up to see the apostles and presbyters in Jerusalem about this question (Acts 14:26—15:2).

Was Simeon among those who went up? It seems quite likely. At Jerusalem Luke records first Peter's speech, then Barnabas' and Paul's account of the conversion of the Gentiles. What more natural than that following this description of somewhat controversial missionary work Simeon, respected both at Antioch and Jerusalem, should sum up the position in the whole Christian Church of Antioch and her daughters? But did he? Luke next mentions James' speech: 'Listen, brethren, to what I have to say. Simeon has told us, how for the first time God has looked with favour on the Gentiles, and chosen from among them a people dedicated to his name' (Acts 15:14). It has been generally presumed that 'Simeon' means St Peter, but Professor Giet of Strasburg has recently brought forward various reasons for doubting this.[1] He thinks that St Peter's words refer to the situation at Caesarea on the conversion of Cornelius (Acts 10), Simeon's—as quoted by James—to that at Antioch. Moreover nowhere else in the New Testament is St

[1] Giet, 'L'Assemblée Apostolique et le Décret de Jérusalem. Qui Etait Siméon?' *Mélanges Jules Lebreton*, I, pp. 203–20.

Peter called 'Simeon'. The Simeon referred to by James would then be a delegate from Antioch, probably Simeon the Black. In fact, if I am right in my earlier surmises, Simeon would have been almost the first Christian to preach openly and successfully to the Gentiles, and no one could more fittingly have made the remarks quoted by St James.

Of course much of this is guess-work, but none of it is unlikely and it does fit well together. We can at least be fairly sure that Luke learnt much from the elders of the Church of Antioch, including most probably the story of St Stephen's passion, and that among those elders were Cyreneans in a particularly favourable position to provide him with such information.

Doubtless Luke had many other sources of whom I have not spoken: Cleophas, perhaps, for the events on the road to Emmaus, and others who will ever remain unnamed. Yet of some at least of that group of eye-witnesses and ministers of the word, who stood behind Luke in the writing of his gospel and receive that rather general acknowledgement in his first lines, we can feel fairly sure. Apart from the writings of Mark, Matthew and the unknown Jerusalem author, there were John and James, at once eye-witnesses and ministers; there was Paul, who was a supreme minister of the word, and a witness— if not perhaps in Luke's sense an eye-witness; there was Philip, again not an eye-witness, but a strenuous and respected evangelical minister; and others, among them the subject of the next chapter, who were eye-witnesses but hardly accredited word ministers. There they all are, contributing each his bit to the stuff of the third gospel: a patchwork indeed, but a patchwork rendered into a single coherent and highly exciting piece of work by the mind of its author.

4

JOANNA, THE WIFE OF CHUSA, HEROD'S STEWARD

A LESS renowned but not less valuable source for St Luke than those considered in the last chapter was, I feel, Joanna, the wife of Chusa, a certain eye-witness of the Gospel events. We know little about her—only two brief references in the third gospel (8:3; 24:10). Even this is significant. Why did Luke bother to mention her? Her name was ignored in the earlier gospels, and Luke's apparent anxiety to name her in his would be well explained if she was one of the sources of his information. This, which has often been suggested before, is far from an airy hypothesis, for Joanna was certainly in a position to provide much of that special information which Luke did actually come to possess from some unnamed source.

Here then are the passages which tell us about Joanna:

> Then followed a time in which he went on journeying from one city or village to another, preaching and spreading the good news of God's kingdom. With him were the twelve apostles, and certain women, whom he had freed from evil spirits and from sicknesses, Mary who is called Magdalen, who had had seven devils cast out of her, and Joanna, the wife of Chusa, Herod's steward, and Susanna, and many others, who ministered to him with the means they had (8:1-3).

Immediately after describing the Crucifixion and death of our Lord, Luke continues:

All his acquaintances, with the women who had followed him from Galilee, watched while this happened, standing at a distance. And now a man called Joseph came forward. . . . He it was who approached Pilate, and asked to have the body of Jesus. This he took, and wrapped it in a winding-sheet, and laid it in a tomb fashioned out of the rock, in which no man had ever been buried. It was the day of preparation; the next day was the sabbath. And the women who had come with him from Galilee followed, and saw the tomb, and how his body was buried; so they went back, and prepared spices and ointments, and while it was the sabbath they kept still, as the law commanded.

And at very early dawn on the first day of the week they came to the tomb, bringing the spices they had prepared: and found the stone already rolled away from the door of the tomb. They went into it, and could not find the body of the Lord Jesus. They were still puzzling over this when two men came and stood by them, in shining garments. These said to them, as they bowed their faces to the earth in fear, Why are you seeking one who is alive, here among the dead? He is not here, he has risen again; remember how he told you, while he was still in Galilee, the Son of Man is to be given up into the hands of sinners, and to be crucified, and to rise again the third day. Then they remembered what he had said, and returned from the tomb bringing news of all this to the eleven apostles and to all the rest. It was Mary Magdalen, and Joanna, and Mary the mother of James, and the other women that were with them,[1] who told the apostles this; but to their minds the story seemed madness, and they could not believe it (23:49—24:11).

[1] This most important phrase is unaccountably omitted in the Knox translation.

These texts tell us three things about Joanna:

1. She was freed by Jesus from diabolical possession or sickness, and was subsequently one of those women who ministered to him during his public life.

2. She was one of those who witnessed the Crucifixion and went to the tomb on the morning of the Resurrection.

3. She was from Galilee, and was the wife of Herod's steward, Chusa.

I will take these one by one.

1. She was one of those who ministered to Jesus, and hence most certainly heard much of his teaching. The apostles apart, the holy women must have been the most continuous, and surely assiduous, witnesses of Jesus' public life and teaching. The angels tell us that the holy women had themselves heard Jesus' predictions of his Crucifixion and Resurrection (24:6), and these predictions were part of the more secret teaching of Jesus; they were then reliable witnesses of the whole public ministry. Now it is precisely such a witness that we seek as source for the information contained in Luke's central section, 9:51—18:14, describing events and teaching which seem to have had little place in the original apostolic catechesis. The first two gospels were chiefly concerned to give a written version of that oral teaching, but St Luke, in contrast, was writing a biography, for which the established catechesis was only one source. Maybe the events and teaching peculiar to his gospel happened mainly while the apostles, or at any rate St Peter,[1] were absent, perhaps on the Palestinian mission. But the holy women are not likely to have left Jesus for long, and they—Joanna in particular—may well be Luke's source for at least some of the facts recorded in his central section.

[1] The only mention of St Peter in Luke's central section is in 12:41, which is common to Matthew.

2. Joanna was one of the holy women who witnessed the Crucifixion and discovered the empty tomb on Easter morning. Luke, it is true, only names her explicitly as a witness to the empty tomb and the vision of angels; but there is clear continuity between 'the women who had followed him from Galilee' standing on Calvary (23:49), the women from Galilee [1] who saw the tomb where Joseph laid the body of Jesus, and who then prepared spices (23:55–6), the women who came to that tomb with the spices they had prepared (24:1) and there had a vision of angels, and finally the women, among whom was Joanna, who brought news of this to the apostles.

Joanna was a witness to the Passion and the Resurrection, and with Mary Magdalen she brought the good news to the apostles themselves. She witnessed to the witnesses, evangelized the apostles.

Between them, the four evangelists name four of the women as witnesses of the angelic apparitions on Easter morning: Mary Magdalen (all four gospels); 'the other Mary', the mother of James (all three synoptics); Salome (Mark); and Joanna (Luke). But according to Luke's explicit statement there was an unspecified number of others, unnamed. If, in the third gospel, Joanna leaves the group of the unnamed, it is because she had for Luke some special importance, and if not in the events themselves, then probably in their narration. The different accounts which we have of the events of that morning can be in part explained as deriving from different women; in which case, Luke's narrative may enshrine Joanna's account of the Easter morning events and contain her contribution to the gospel of the redemption.

[1] Perhaps this stress on 'the women *from Galilee*' (23:49 and 55), so effectively faithful to the Lord, is in implied contrast with the 'daughters of Jerusalem' (23:28) whose affective weeping was rebuked by Jesus.

3. The hypothesis which makes of Joanna one important source for Luke's special information seems of most value when we come to consider his knowledge of Herod. Luke was very well-informed about Herod, far more so than the other evangelists; it is more than likely that he is dropping a deliberate hint about the source of this information when he tells us that Joanna was the wife of Herod's steward. Knowledge of this possible source is the more valuable to us on account of those critics, among them Loisy, who deny that Jesus was ever taken before Herod at all.

Herod Antipas, a son of Herod the Great, was tetrarch of Galilee and Peraea from 4 B.C. until A.D. 39. In the latter year he was deposed by Rome and retired into exile in Gaul. Apart from chapters 1 and 2 of Matthew, where of course his father, Herod the Great, is spoken of, all the Gospel references to Herod are to Herod the tetrarch. His name appears four times in Matthew, ten in Mark, and thirteen in Luke. It is worth considering these references.

Matthew and Mark both tell the story of John the Baptist's imprisonment and martyrdom at length (Mt. 14:1–12; Mk. 6:14–29). This accounts for all the references to Herod Antipas in Matthew and all but three in Mark.[1] Luke on the other hand only mentions Herod's dealings with St John in passing in 3:19–20 and 9:9. While the first two gospels treat of the Baptist's martyrdom as something of importance and interest in itself, St Luke is only concerned with it as throwing

---

[1] Mark's other three references to Herod (Mk. 3:6; 8:15–16; 12:13) are to 'Herod's party' and to 'the leaven of Herod'. Evidently these refer to a group of Jews comparable with the Pharisees and the Sadducees; these passages tell us about Jesus' ministry and the factions he had to face, but nothing about Herod himself.

light on the relationship between Herod and Jesus, with which the first two evangelists were not concerned. This fits in with Luke's whole treatment of St John. He starts with a detailed account of the Precursor's birth and preaching; then suddenly after 3:20 John fades out of the picture. It is not even explicitly stated that he baptized Jesus. Luke's interest in John is wholly due to his function of prophet inaugurating the messianic age. Herein lies the significance of John's preaching, hence its solemn dating. In this Luke may be much influenced by his source; but the interest of the third gospel in John, as in Herod, is clearly not historical or biographical: John's theological function performed, he is ruthlessly removed from the picture. Luke's treatment of St Peter in Acts is worth comparing.

As the facts of John's martyrdom were certainly well known, the passages referring to it do not suggest any particularly close knowledge of Herod himself, nor any special interest in him. They are focused on John, not on Herod, nor on the relations between Jesus and Herod. With Luke it is quite different. Nine of the thirteen mentions of Herod's name in the third gospel give us new and interesting information about him,[1] and must now be given in full, together with one passage not mentioning Herod, but of importance for our subject.

9:7–9. And Herod, who was prince in that quarter, heard of all his doings, and did not know what to think, some telling him that John had risen from the dead, and some that Elias had appeared, and some that one of the old prophets had returned to life. John, said Herod, I beheaded; who can this be, of whom I hear such reports? And he was eager to see him.

[1] The other four are: Lk. 3:1; 8:3; 3:19–20.

13:1–3. At this very time there were some present that told him the story of those Galileans, whose blood Pilate had shed in the midst of their sacrifices. And Jesus said in answer, Do you suppose because this befell them, that these men were worse sinners than all else in Galilee? I tell you it is not so; you will all perish as they did, if you do not repent.

13:31–3. It was on that day that some of the Pharisees came to him and said, Go elsewhere, and leave this place; Herod has a mind to kill thee. And he said to them, Go and tell that fox, Behold, to-day and to-morrow I am to continue casting out devils, and doing works of healing; it is on the third day that I am to reach my consummation. But to-day and to-morrow and the next day I must go on my journeys; there is no room for a prophet to meet his death, except at Jerusalem.

23:4–12. Pilate said to the chief priests and the multitudes, I cannot discover any fault in this man. But they insisted, He rouses sedition among the people; he has gone round the whole of Judaea preaching, beginning in Galilee and ending here. Pilate, upon the mention of Galilee, asked whether the man was a Galilean; and learning that he belonged to Herod's jurisdiction, remitted his cause to Herod, who was also in Jerusalem at this time. Herod was overjoyed at seeing Jesus; for a long time he had been eager to have sight of him, because he had heard so much of him, and now he hoped to witness some miracle of his. He asked him many questions, but could get no answer from him, although the chief priests and scribes stood there, loudly accusing him. So Herod and his attendants made a jest of him, arraying him in festal attire out of mockery, and sent him back to Pilate. That day Herod and Pilate, who had hitherto been at enmity with one another, became friends.

We have here a very interesting sequence of information in which the earlier passages quite plainly lead up to and prepare for the account of Jesus' trial before Herod. The historicity of the latter is further supported by an interesting reference in the Acts—4:23–8.

> Now that they were set free, they went back to their company, and told them all the chief priests and elders had said. And they, when they heard it, uttered prayer to God with one accord; Ruler of all, thou art the maker of heaven and earth and the sea, and all that is in them. Thou hast said through thy holy Spirit, by the lips of thy servant David, our father, What means this turmoil among the nations; why do the peoples cherish vain dreams? See how the kings of the earth stand in array, how its rulers make common cause, against the Lord and his Christ. True enough, in this city of ours, Herod and Pontius Pilate, with the Gentiles and the people of Israel to aid them, made common cause against thy holy servant Jesus, so accomplishing all that thy power and wisdom had decreed.

If this passage well confirms Luke's gospel narrative, its own historical character is vouched for by the really archaic character of the whole prayer: it is a perfect example of the most primitive Christian thought and spirituality.

The source of our first passage 9:7–9 is clearly the parallel passage in Mark 6:14–16. But what is significant in the Lucan version is the last line (no parallel in Mark): 'And he was eager to see him.' This obviously links up with 23:8. 'Herod was overjoyed at seeing Jesus; for a long time he had been eager to have sight of him.'

If this was one aspect of Herod's attitude towards Jesus—one of patronizing, suspicious and superstitious curiosity (his approach to John was much the same, cf. Mark 6:20)—Jesus' attitude to Herod was one of sheer rejection and indifference. 'Go and tell that fox, Behold, to-day and to-morrow I am to continue casting out devils, and doing works of healing; it is on the third day that I am to reach my consummation.' Hence faced with Herod's questioning Jesus would not answer a word; 'that fox' was representative in Jerusalem neither of Caesar, as was Pilate, nor of the Old Law, as was the High Priest. In the curiosity of John the Baptist's murderer Jesus was not interested: 'He asked him many questions, but could get no answer from him.'

As for the reference in 13:1–3 to the massacre of some Galileans 'in the midst of their sacrifices'—evidently then in the temple of Jerusalem: Galileans were Herod's subjects, and their slaughter by Pilate while on pilgrimage to Jerusalem must surely have angered the tetrarch. At least the incident goes to explain the enmity which Luke tells us existed between the two (23:12). But it also helps us to understand other aspects of Jesus' trial. 'Pilate, upon the mention of Galilee, asked whether the man was a Galilean; and learning that he belonged to Herod's jurisdiction, remitted his cause to Herod, who was also in Jerusalem at this time.' Pilate's recognition of Herod's jurisdiction over a Galilean, entirely ignored in the previous case, may well have been due to a desire to disembarrass himself in an awkward situation, and perhaps also to set Herod and the priests in conflict. But Herod was nevertheless pleased by this act of deference. And though he did not care to involve himself in the case—John's death had surely already earned him sufficient unpopularity—he clearly sympathized with Pilate and the two, as Luke tells us, became friends from that day.

Herod then hoped to avoid responsibility for Jesus' death. At first sight this might seem hardly in accord with what we read in 13:31–2: 'Some of the Pharisees came to him and said, Go elsewhere, and leave this place; Herod has a mind to kill thee.' But this statement probably revealed much more the mind of the Pharisees than the mind of Herod. Moreover the latter was not ruler in Jerusalem, and was probably only too glad to see the high priests and Pilate earning disfavour with the people through their treatment of the latest popular prophet. He at least would rather mock than condemn. This accords with all we know of Antipas; he only reluctantly consented to the Baptist's execution, while the character that Josephus draws is, in Lagrange's words, that of 'a prudent ruler, friendly to everybody, when not led astray by his wife or besotted by wine'.[1]

But did Herod then avoid his share of responsibility for Jesus' martyrdom? Hardly. The day of the Crucifixion was the day he became friends with Pontius Pilate. Like the latter, he was one of the princes, one of the kings of the earth, who conspired together against the Lord and His Christ that day in Jerusalem. And this is very much part of Luke's theme. Pilate too, no doubt, had his good points, but that does not excuse him from being part of that Jerusalem which was 'still murdering the prophets, and stoning the messengers that are sent to thee' (13:34). They were both part of the generation that 'will be answerable for all the blood of prophets that has been shed since the beginning of the world' (11:50). And this because Jesus was himself a prophet, *the* prophet, and 'there is no room for a prophet to meet his death, except at Jerusalem' (13:33). But at Jerusalem it was fitting that Herod of Galilee, murderer of the last and greatest of the Old Testament prophets, should be present to join with Pilate and the chief priests in doing to death Jesus the Galilean. The early Christians had no doubt of Herod's guilt, for when they summed up

[1] Lagrange, *Gospel of Jesus Christ*, I, p. 218.

the enemies of Jesus they put him first of all: 'In this city of ours, Herod and Pontius Pilate, with the Gentiles and the people of Israel to aid them, made common cause against thy holy servant Jesus.'

Thus Luke's series of passages forms a unity; the early ones explain the later, and the whole gives us a theme running through the gospel. This theme in its turn links up with the much bigger and more important one of Jesus as a prophet, the heir of the Old Testament prophets, and destined as such to meet his death in Jerusalem where all the murderers of the prophets came together to destroy him.

We must return to the question of sources. There is no reason to suggest that all Luke's Herodian material came from Joanna: as already seen, much of one passage is a borrowing from Mark. Yet it seems very likely that at least the facts concerning Jesus' interview with Herod are owed to Joanna. Evidently the apostles, while aware that Jesus was sent to Herod by Pilate, knew little of what had occurred during this interlude; otherwise it would surely not have been ignored by the other gospels. This is not surprising: it was not a public trial, not strictly a trial at all, and the apostles were not likely to have been present. Information on what had happened would come most naturally from one within the circle of Herod's court, and who then more likely than the wife of his steward?[1]

It is possible that Luke did not receive Joanna's story from her own lips: she would have been very old, if still alive, by the time he was making his gospel notes. But Luke came from

[1] B. H. Streeter has already suggested this, cf. 'On the Trial of Our Lord before Herod: a Suggestion' in *Oxford Studies in the Synoptic Problem* (ed. W. Sanday), pp. 229–31.

Antioch and among the prophets and teachers of the Church there was Manahen, foster-brother of Herod the tetrarch (Acts 13:1). Dom John Chapman suggested that Joanna was Herod's foster-mother and Manahen's mother[1]; it is anyway probable that her information came to Luke through Manahen, and was perhaps as much his as hers. This would be just another instance of Luke's debt to the elders of the Church at Antioch.

Once he was provided with accurate information about Jesus' appearance before Herod, he could emphasize their earlier relations in order to throw light upon this final scene. How he obtained the various pieces of information does not matter much; what is important is his use of them within the key themes of his gospel. Thus considered they assume a real significance, and are far from being mere snippets of additional information almost unconnected with Luke's central preoccupations. If Luke owed much of this Herodian material, together with other information, to Joanna, the wife of Chusa, and to Manahen—and it is highly probable that he did—then we owe them a debt which the briefness of their explicit appearances in Holy Scripture must not allow us to forget.

[1] Chapman, *Matthew, Mark and Luke*, p. 173.

4

A GREAT PROPHET HAS RISEN UP AMONG US

'It is only in his own country, in his own home that a prophet goes unhonoured.'[1] This was Jesus' comment on his home reception in Nazareth, an event placed significantly by Luke at the very opening of the public ministry. After so many years during which there had been no prophet in Israel, in which the very idea of a prophet had, for the more orthodox, become part of the past rather than the present, there was again a living prophet. The common testimony of the synoptics leaves no doubt that Jesus used the title, though it was not his favourite way of describing himself; he is called the same in the very earliest apostolic witness—Acts 3:22; 7:37—and this too would be difficult to explain if the name had not first been used by Jesus himself. There is moreover a whole host of texts to demonstrate that it was above all as a prophet that the common people received him; the Samaritan woman's 'Sir, I perceive that thou art a prophet' (Jn. 4:19) was the normal reaction to his teaching and miracles. In the first gospel this is particularly clear; when he entered Jerusalem before the last Pasch the

[1] Mt. 13:57; Mk. 6:4; Lk. 4:24. Jesus again describes himself as a prophet in Luke 13:33. It is an inadequate explanation of these texts to say that he was *merely* quoting proverbs. For a lively treatment of Jesus as prophet see P. Daniélou, *Advent* (Sheed & Ward, 1950), pp. 157–81.

whole city was disturbed: 'Who is this? they asked. And the multitude answered, This is Jesus, the prophet from Nazareth in Galilee' (Mt. 21:11). The chief priests and pharisees, we are told, would gladly have laid hands on him, but they feared the people who looked upon him as a prophet (Mt. 21:46). Our Lord's prophetical character was then an accepted thing in his own lifetime and in the primitive church.[1] It was an idea which Luke developed, but to understand it properly we have first to turn back to the prophets of the Old Testament. [2]

In the first book of Samuel (9:9) we read that 'He who is now called a Prophet, in time past was called a Seer'. The first word, the one used most often in the Old Testament to describe prophets, is in Hebrew *nābî*, the second *rō'eh*. From these two words we can obtain some idea of what a prophet was. Let us take *rō'eh* first; he was a seer, one who saw further and deeper than others. Through visions, or better still vision, he could get beyond the world normally presented to our senses, and divine reality was revealed to him. In the Lamentations of Jeremias it is written that 'Israel's prophets have found no vision from the Lord' (2:9); they lacked in fact their essential

[1] The full list of non-Lucan references to Christ as a prophet may be given here: Mt. 13:57; 16:14; 21:11,46. Mk. 6:4,15; 8:28. Jn. 4:19; 6:14; 7:40, 52; 9:17.

[2] For fuller treatment of the Old Testament background and massive bibliographies, I may refer to E. F. Sutcliffe, S.J., in his article 'Prophetical Literature' in *A Catholic Commentary on Holy Scripture*, pp. 527–38; O. Eissfeldt's chapter with the same title in *The Old Testament and Modern Study* (Oxford, 1951), pp. 115–61; J. Giblet's study of 'Prophétisme et Attente d'un Messie-prophète dans le Judaisme', in *L'Attente du Messie*, pp. 85–130; and the chapter on 'Revelation and the Unconscious' (pp. 107–40) in Victor White O.P., *God and the Unconscious* (Harvill, 1952).

gift, had become tasteless salt. But to have vision was never the whole story of a prophet; he was not only one who saw things, but one who proclaimed what he saw, and that brings us to the second name—*nābī*. The origin of the word is not known but its sense can be had fairly well from two passages in Exodus. The Lord told Moses to take Aaron as his spokesman, 'Speak to him, and put my words in his mouth; and I will be in thy mouth, and in his mouth, and will show you what you must do. He shall speak in thy stead to the people, and shall be thy mouth but thou shalt be to him in those things that pertain to God' (Ex. 4:15–16). And again the Lord said to Moses, 'Behold I have appointed thee the God of Pharao: and Aaron thy brother shall be thy prophet' (Ex. 7:1). Evidently it is the same thing to be someone's prophet or their mouth, that is to say spokesman and interpreter. A prophet is one who speaks; the word is his characteristic (see Jer. 18:18). But it is not his own word that he utters, because he is called, inspired by God, and then 'sent' to speak in God's name to the people.

These are the two sides of the prophet's character: the passive, recipient side, that of the seer granted the enlightenment of contemplation; and then the active, vocal side, the mission of preaching. Personally called and taken into the hidden counsels of God, enabled to see something of the divine ways which are not human ways, the prophet is then sent back to his fellow men to proclaim to them the divine way, path of righteousness and salvation, the kingdom of heaven. The divine sending of the true prophet is essential, and his temporal mission is the pre-figurement of that of Jesus the prophet-Son. 'Since the days that your fathers came forth out of the land of Egypt unto this day I have ever sent unto you all my servants the prophets, daily rising up early and sending them.'[1] Thus the true prophet combined vision with mission.

In fulfilling this mission he proved his authority by signs and miracles. Some prophets like Moses and Elias were great miracle workers, others in the conventional sense were not, but all in one way or another had the manifest power of God upon them. This power was their authentication, but miracles and prophecies as such remained subsidiary to their primary function which was moral and doctrinal, the proclamation of God's ways to men. This proclamation was made in a multitude of ways, some of which must seem to us bizarre and obscure rather than enlightening. What is most strange is the insertion of the supernatural within the realms of the ordinary or the fantasy of the psychic, the religious significance of 'a hook to draw down fruit' (Amos 8:2) or of Nabuchodonosor's dreams. The effect of divine insight could well be overwhelming; human flesh is not made for such experience, and at times no other response may seem possible than Jeremias' 'I cannot speak for I am a child' (Jer. 1:6). Revelation was rich and diverse both in its content and its mode, and could as well be made on the purely intellectual level as mediated through a vision, dream or just a sudden intuition. This psychological side of prophetism is important, especially for the prophets of the earlier period of Israelite history. There were always many more who had the psychological than who had the theological character of prophet: the 'schools of prophets' and the 'sons of the prophets' represented a certain natural gift of prophecy, not easily distinguishable from the strictly supernatural calling; they shared the same outward phenomena and served to point out the true interpreter of the word of God.

[1] Jer. 7:25; see also Jer. 23:21; Judges 6:8; 2 Chron. 24:19; 25:15.

The history of prophetism in Israel is nearly identical with the history of the chosen people itself, from Moses, like whom 'there arose no more a prophet in Israel' (Deut. 34:10), through Nathan and Elias, Amos, Isaias and Jeremias, to the time when there was not only no prophet like unto Moses, but no prophet at all—'there was no prophet in Israel' (1 Mach. 9:27). It was a sign that the old dispensation was nearing its close.

Moses was the great foundation figure for Israel, the man who had led the tribes throughout Exodus, Israel's springtime of testing and the classical moment of her relationship with God. In a way he hardly belongs to the prophetical tradition, which is characteristic of a later period. Nevertheless he was canonized as the greatest of prophets, as the man who had had the closest vision of God (on Sinai) and who beyond all others had been the interpreter of the will of God to his people. Of him alone was it said that 'The Lord spoke to Moses face to face as a man is accustomed to speak to his friend' (Ex. 33:11); and he alone was law-giver, mediate source of that law which grew to embrace practically the whole of Jewish religion. Israel was agreed that no more recent figure could be compared with him, and that makes it all the more strange that Deuteronomy foretells the coming of a new Moses, like unto the first. This is a prophecy of high importance. After rules for priests and levites and the forbidding of soothsayers Moses continued:

Thou shalt be perfect: and without spot before the Lord thy God. These nations, whose land thou shalt possess, hearken to sooth-sayers and divines: but thou art otherwise instructed by the Lord thy God. The Lord thy God will raise up to thee a prophet of thy nation and of thy brethren like unto me. Him thou shalt hear. As thou desiredst of the Lord thy God in Horeb, when the assembly was gathered together, and saidst: Let me not hear any more the voice of the Lord my God, neither let me see any more this exceeding great fire, lest I die. And the Lord said to me: They have spoken all things well. I will raise them up a prophet out of the midst of their brethren like to thee. And I will put my words in his mouth: and he shall speak to them all that I shall command him. And he that will not hear his words, which he shall speak in my name, I will be the revenger. But the prophet, who being corrupted with pride, shall speak in my name things that I did not command him to say, or in the name of strange gods, shall be slain. And if in silent thought thou answer: How shall I know the word that the Lord hath not spoken? Thou shalt have this sign: Whatsoever that same prophet foretelleth in the name of the Lord, and it cometh not to pass; that thing the Lord hath not spoken, but the prophet hath forged it by the pride of his mind. And therefore thou shalt not fear him (Deut. 18:13–22).

We have here the classical account of the prophet's role in Israel; though speaking of a single prophet it clearly refers to the 'institution' of prophets, of a series of men raised up by God to continue Moses' work of speaking to Israel in the name of God; a single prophet would not have answered the purpose as indicated by the people's request at Horeb. The reference to false prophets points to the same conclusion. But here as elsewhere a prophecy referring to a whole group has a fuller sense not satisfied by its group explanation.[1] The prophecy's full meaning requires not only a series of prophets, but also a single one who, summing up all in himself, will be great as Moses both in closeness to God and as legislator for God's people.

Next to Moses stands Elias, a figure still more enigmatic; no one surely is more distant, more difficult to comprehend.

[1] Nathan's prophecy to David, 2 Samuel 7:5–17, and the prophecy of the Son of Man in Daniel 7 are other examples.

'Prophet and father of prophets' St Ephraem called him, and
St Jerome thought him the type of all prophets.[1] He is a truly
archetypal figure to be encountered in religion's deepest places
like the desert and the Order of Carmelites, but in life it was
his fierce opposition to idolatry which was his most striking
characteristic, a perennial struggle with the Baal worship of
Queen Jezabel of Samaria. He wrote not a word, but his
miracles, his power with God to bring down rain and fire to
earth, to raise the dead or massacre the enemies of true religion
was prodigious. And then, like Moses, he 'saw' God (3 Kings
19:13), and just in that place where Moses too had seen Him, on
Mount Horeb or Sinai. Finally Elias did not die but was carried
up to heaven in a chariot; and not dying, he became a symbol
of immortality, life beyond the grave, the Resurrection. His
return as precursor of the Messiah was prophesied by Malachy
and constantly expected by the Jews of later times.

'This, then, was the testimony which John bore, when the
Jews sent priests and Levites from Jerusalem, to ask him, Who
art thou? He admitted the truth, without concealment; admitted that he was not the Christ. What then, they asked him,
art thou Elias? Not Elias, he said. Art thou the prophet? And
he answered, No.' (Jn. 1:19–21). Here we see the variety of
ideas in Our Lord's time about the 'coming one'—the Messiah,
Elias, the prophet. Expectation of the latter seems to have been
due less to Deuteronomy than to contemporary eschatological
nationalism. The common people, unlike the scribes and
pharisees, had never reconciled themselves to the extinction of
the prophetic gift in Israel, and even the Maccabees had been

---

[1] For a breathtakingly comprehensive treatment of Elias, see the two
volumes of *Elie Le Prophète, Les Etudes Carmélitaines* (Desclée De
Brouwer, 1956).

thought of as prophets (they were already priests and kings). Since their time the expectation of an approaching prophet was mixed up with the nationalist messianism then rampant. Such men as Theodas and Judas the Galilean, mentioned by Gamaliel (Acts 5:36–7), were readily received as prophets by the common people; and the return of Elias, greatest of all wonder-workers, was anxiously awaited. If there seems to have been little explicit expectation of a prophet-messiah, the explanation may be partly that people were less concerned with the coming of a personal messiah than with that of the messianic age, and partly that prophet and messiah were still normally distinguished: the prophet's coming was to be the immediate sign of messianic times, which he would usher in, preparing the way for the messiah-king who would follow. This expectation of the prophet-precursor was remarkably vindicated, as the first chapters of St Luke especially indicate, in the preaching of John, son of Zachary.

It was certainly the popular expectation of a powerful prophet of one kind or another which explains Jesus' tremendous welcome by the common people. John's preaching had already drawn vast crowds, and at first sight Jesus seemed to fulfil still better all the yearnings of popular Jewish religion for a prophet or messiah-king. Only slowly did they realize how different he was from what they had come to expect and desire. The early Church interpreted his prophetical function much less according to the popular apocalyptic ideas of the time than in the classical terms of Deuteronomy 18, and seems (with maybe the Samaritans) to have been the first to understand the latter in a fully messianic sense. Here as elsewhere the root of Christian theology is to be found in Jesus' bringing together of different strands of Old Testament teaching and prophecy in his own person.[1] The prophet of Deuteronomy, unlike some of the later popular conceptions of the future prophet, had his feet firmly planted on earth; and yet Jesus was able to link this up in himself with the Son of Man 'coming on the clouds of heaven'; his teaching about himself was a revolutionary combination of Old Testament ideas, reconcilable only in the light of his own personality.

But more important than Deuteronomy 18 for Jesus' own conception of his prophetical character is another set of texts, that of the suffering servant of the Lord, described by Deutero-Isaias.[2] The figure of the servant depicted is that of a prophet, a prophet in some ways very like Moses; it was especially as the servant of the Lord that Jesus manifested himself, a prophet representative of his people, and one that had to pass through suffering to glory. It is in these texts that the coming was revealed of the

> Man of sorrows and acquainted with infirmity: and his look was as it were hidden and despised. Whereupon we esteemed him not. Surely he hath borne our infirmities and carried our sorrows: and we have thought him as it were a leper, and as one struck by God and afflicted. But he was wounded for our iniquities: he was bruised for our sins. The chastisement of our peace was upon him: and by his bruises we are healed (Isa. 53:3–5).

[1] Old Testament theology presents a complex of converging lines; separate in the Old Testament they all come to meet in Jesus. But some had already drawn together in pre-Christian times. Thus as we have noticed the Maccabees were priests and kings, and some also attributed to them something of the prophetic character. 'The Master of Justice' of the Damascus sect was both a messianic and a prophetic figure (see Giblet, pp. 125–8). The Servant of the Lord of Deutero-Isaias was also given both royal and prophetical characteristics. (See V. de Leeuw, 'Le Serviteur de Jahvé Figure Royale ou prophétique', *L'Attente du Messie*, pp. 51–6.)

[2] The four so-called 'Songs of the Servant of the Lord' are to be found in Isaias 42:1–9; 49:1–7; 50:4–9; 52:13—53:12.

Although these passages were interpreted messianically even before our Lord,[1] the people of his time were certainly expecting a glorious rather than a suffering messiah; the need for his sufferings was the burden of most of the teaching given by Jesus to his closest disciples, yet it was also what they found most difficult to understand. In spite of his frequent prophecies they were overwhelmed by the Passion, and only after the Resurrection did they understand the teaching he had given them about his redemptive death. And this teaching made use above all of the Servant songs in Isaias; the New Testament is saturated with references to them. This was common Christian teaching, St Luke's included, and he gives us its *locus classicus* in his account of Philip and the eunuch in Acts 8 : 30–5 ; but it is also true that St Luke speaks less of Jesus' sufferings than Matthew or Mark, and he toned down their picture of the Passion, concentrating more on the glory. It was St Peter himself who best understood the mystery of Jesus' suffering, Peter who previously had failed to accept it at all (Mk. 8:32–3); but having once understood he never forgot it, and the theology of Jesus' sufferings, of Jesus the suffering servant, is pre-eminently his.[2]

The aspect of the Servant songs which probably appealed most to Luke was their universalism. The servant 'will bring forth judgment to the Gentiles' (42:1), he is given 'for a covenant of the people, for a light of the Gentiles' (42:6). Called from the womb God says to him, 'Thou art my servant Israel, for in thee will I glory. . . . Behold I have given thee to be the light of the Gentiles, that thou mayest be my salvation even to the

[1] See H. Hegermann, *Jesaja 53 in Hexapla, Targum und Peschitta*, 1954.

[2] See V. Taylor, 'The Origin of the Markan Passion Sayings', *New Testament Studies*, 1, 3, pp. 159–67; S. Garofalo, 'Pietro "testimone" della passione', *Euntes Docete*, III, 2, pp. 181–206.

farthest part of the earth' (49:3, 6). All of which was fulfilled
in Jesus, 'the light which shall give revelation to the Gentiles,
the glory of thy people Israel' (Lk. 2:32). By many other little
traits Luke further delineates Jesus as the prophetic servant of
the Lord, who would be called from the womb, on whom the
Spirit would rest, who would give law and justice, inaugurate
a new age, and suffer for the sins of his people. But in speaking
of Luke we are anticipating, and for a moment we must return
to sum up the pre-Lucan position.

Behind Jesus, prophet-messiah, there was a vast and complex
prophetical tradition, which we even now do not understand
too well. It was a cord of many different strands, weaving and
inter-weaving, and preparing for Jesus' use at once the classical
prophecy of the Deuteronomic prophet, the mysterious messianic figure of the suffering servant of the Lord, and other
popular and less orthodox ideas, which were very widely
spread among the Jews of Jesus' time. Yet combined with this
expectation of a prophet was the sad reality that for long there
had been no prophet in Israel. When the prophetical tradition
had thus died out, the appearance of a new prophet inevitably
implied something more than a continuation of the prophets of
the past, it suggested the arrival of a new epoch, the messianic
age. As we have seen, both Jesus and the early Church made
use of this expectation and these ideas, and St Luke had a firm
foundation on which to build. To him we now return, to
consider his interpretation of the Old Testament witness and
New Testament fulfilment woven into the pattern of his
teaching.

The first prophet to appear in the third gospel, as in the
other gospels, is John the Baptist. He was the prophet who was
to precede the Messiah and usher in the last age. 'And thou, my

child, wilt be known for a prophet of the most High.'[1] It is because he is a prophet that he will be filled with the Holy Spirit (1:15) and will be supremely a man of prayer and a desert-dweller (1:80), for these were all prophetic traits. The reference to the desert is especially significant: 'He dwelt in the wilderness until the day when he was made manifest to Israel.' The desert was the place where prophets belonged, at least in their formative years—Moses, Elias, and now John the Baptist and then Jesus himself; it was where they were prepared and where they prayed; Jesus was there for forty days before the beginning of the ministry (and maybe for much longer periods previously) and he returned there during the ministry—'he would steal away from them into the desert and pray there' (5:16).

The Jerusalem document constituting the core of Luke's first two chapters brought out sharply John's Elianic character. There was a strong tradition on the subject of Elias' return to earth, as witness the canonical Book of Malachy, the Book of Henoch and 4 Esdras. Our Lord and all primitive Christianity understood this to be fulfilled in John, as we see already in Matthew and Mark. The Jerusalem booklet stressed this point. In it is related how the angel Gabriel told Zachary that John was to prepare the way for the Lord God, 'ushering in his advent in the spirit and power of an Elias' (1:17); Gabriel's description of the work John was to do, 'He shall unite the hearts of all, the fathers with the children', is a clear reference to Elias' role as foretold in Malachy 4:6 and Ecclesiasticus 48:10. Quite certainly Luke was aware of this, and knew that his readers would be aware of it as well. Yet beyond it he avoids mention of John's role of new Elias,

[1] 1:76; see also 7:26; 20:6.

and nowhere makes an explicit identification of one with the other. He omits, clearly deliberately, the conversation given by Matthew and Mark immediately following the Transfiguration[1] and also the second part of Jesus' comment on the Baptist, as given in the first gospel, after the mission of the latter's disciples[2]; in both of these Jesus had clearly identified the Baptist with Elias. The reason for this departure from traditional doctrine will soon appear.

Not only the Baptist but all the figures appearing in Luke's first two chapters are prophetical. They are given the gift of the Spirit—the Spirit of prophecy—and their inspired insight into the divine plan of salvation, manifest in the *Benedictus*, the *Magnificat* and the *Nunc Dimittis* can only remind one of the great prophetical songs of the past, the magnificent hymns of Moses, Deborah and Anna, Samuel's mother. Moreover Simeon and Zachary explicitly prophesy future events, while Anna is called a prophetess. Yet all this outburst of prophetic activity is simply introductory to something altogether surpassing the experience of past times: the arrival of the prophet-messiah himself, the Son of God sitting upon the throne of David.

That Jesus is emphatically delineated as a prophet—*the* prophet—in the third gospel is very clear. His birth, baptism and temptation in the desert all suggest it, especially on account of their numerous references to the Spirit, to be considered in the following chapter. It is even clearer in the first Lucan episode of the public ministry, when Jesus takes up the scroll of Isaias in the Nazareth synagogue and in the words of chapter 61:1–2 proclaims himself the servant of the Lord, or

1 Mt. 17:10–13; Mk. 9:10–12.
2 Mt. 11:7–15; Lk. 7:24–30.

whom the Spirit rests, sent to inaugurate the messianic age; and then comments on his reception by his fellow townsmen with the words, 'No prophet finds acceptance in his own country' (4:24). Indeed, this sentence comes near to summing up the whole theme of the third gospel. 'A great prophet has risen up among us' is the popular conclusion from the raising of the son of the widow of Naim (7:16); the doubting Pharisee reasons to himself 'If this man were a prophet' (7:39), while if for Pilate's Roman soldiers Jesus is a mock king, for their Jewish counterparts in the palace of the High Priest he is a false prophet, and 'Come, prophesy' is the tenor of their raillery (22:64). Right to the end of the story it is especially as a prophet that the Lord is described in Luke's gospel, and the disciples on the road to Emmaus cannot describe him better than as the 'prophet whose words and acts had power with God, and with all the people' (24:19).

All the great prophets were very close to God, and Moses even spoke with him 'face to face', but there is no comparison between such transient Old Testament experiences and Jesus' abiding consciousness of his union with his Father: 'None knows what the Son is, except the Father, and none knows what the Father is, except the Son, and those to whom it is the Son's good pleasure to reveal him' (10:22). It was never any effort for Jesus to turn from men to his Father, the effort was rather the other way—to return to those who understood him so little; even on the cross in the last dread moments of his life the profound awareness of the Father's presence remained unimpaired, 'Father, into thy hands I commend my spirit' (23:46). The special revelations of his union with the Father at such moments as his baptism and Transfiguration were simply a breaking into visibility of this constant, abiding state. From the first moment he was God's Son (1:35) and his union with his Father was the root of his whole being.

To this was added his mission, a task of revelation. He was 'sent'[1] as the spokesman of God, and his mission was to open up the way of salvation for men by word and deed, and then himself send the apostles in their turn to teach and continue his prophetical function for all time. He was sent out, according to the first words of his public ministry, 'to preach the gospel to the poor' (4:18), the gospel of the kingdom. 'I must preach the gospel of God's kingdom to the other cities too, it is for this that I was sent' (4:43). The arrival of the kingdom was certainly good news, but it did not offer any sort of an easy time, or worldly paradise; on the contrary, it demanded total renunciation of the world and total love for Christ and one's neighbour:

> Follow me. . . . Leave the dead to bury their dead. . . . Sell what you have, and give alms. . . . (Peter said, and what of us? we have forsaken all that was ours, and followed thee.) . . . It is for thee to go out and proclaim God's kingdom. . . . Love your enemies, do good to those who hate you. . . . Everyone who has forsaken home, or parents, or brethren, or wife, or children for the sake of the kingdom of God, will receive in this present world, many times their worth, and in the world to come, everlasting life.[2]

It was no abstract moral doctrine which Jesus preached, something independent of his own person. No, it was *his* doctrine, *his* commandments; 'follow *me*' is the supreme law and acknowledgement of *him* will be the test in the coming judgment: 'Whoever acknowledges me . . . will be acknowledged,

[1] Lk. 4:18, 43; Acts 3:26.
[2] 9:59, 60; 12:33; 18:28; 9:60; 6:27; 18:29–30.

... he who disowns me ... will be disowned' (12:8-9). The prophets of the past proclaimed the ways of God almost impersonally, but now they are identified with the preacher himself: his present coming has inaugurated the kingdom, his future coming will finally establish it. The public teaching ends with these solemn words: 'Keep watch, then, praying at all times, so that you may be found worthy to come safe through all that lies before you, and stand erect to meet the presence of the Son of Man' (21:36).

Present and future are inextricably mixed in the teaching of Jesus, and every doctrine has meaning in both fields. The future dimension was the more important one; if the kingdom had already made its appearance in his life, its real (if still incomplete) establishment was to come later, after the Passion, the Resurrection and then the Descent of the Spirit. It is only in *Acts* that we find the realization of Jesus' teaching, the fellowship of the kingdom; and this is still not the definitive realization which is dependent on the second coming and judgment. Within the general body of teaching there were some things which related to specific events of the future, the sequence to present events in the ministry: the central issue of Jesus' public life was his relationship with Israel, the chosen people of God, and consequently his specific prophecies of the future concerned this same relationship as worked out in him and in Jerusalem. In the immediate future he prophesied for himself betrayal, suffering, death and resurrection[1]; for Jerusalem her rejection of him and its consequences, her own rejection and destruction.[2] Beyond these, two others intimately linked with them, so much so that it is often not easy to see

[1] 9:22, 44; 18:31-4; etc.
[2] Especially 19:41-4; 21:20-4.

5

which words of his apply to the near and which to the more distant future. Beyond death and resurrection is Jesus' second coming, when the glory and power already revealed in the Resurrection will finally shine out in all their clarity (21:27); beyond the end of Jerusalem is the end of the world when not only will there be tribulation in Judaea but the very powers of heaven will rock (21:26). In both cases the immediate event is the sign, guarantee, and mystical inauguration of the more remote one; the meaning of them is continuous, flowing from one to the other, and Jesus' words hardly distinguish between them because—like all prophecies—they are concerned not with giving historical pre-views with precise chronological divisions, but with pointing out in significant images the divine meaning in the mysteries of the future.

It is in his second coming that Jesus' power (δύναμις) will finally be revealed, but he makes manifest use of it even while on earth. This word 'power' is indeed linked more with his role of earthly prophet, in slight contrast with another word 'authority' (ἐξουσία) which belongs to him more especially as the heavenly Son of Man. His miracles are acts of prophetical power—*dynameis*—by which he exercises compassion, proves his authority and manifests by visible signs the divine mysteries he has come to teach.[1] They are the proofs of his messiahship: 'Go and tell John what your own eyes and ears have witnessed; how the blind see, and the lame walk, and the lepers are made clean, and the deaf hear, how the dead are raised to life, and the poor have the gospel preached to them. Blessed is he who does not lose confidence in me' (7:22–3); thus the programme announced in the synagogue of Nazareth (4:18–19) is fulfilled. Like his whole function of prophet, so his power in

[1] In the Acts miracles often receive the 'Johannine' name of signs (σημεῖα).

particular is connected with the Holy Spirit: 'Jesus came back to Galilee with the power of the Spirit upon him' (4:14). The Holy Spirit and the power of the most High are equated in 1:35; Jesus, Peter told Cornelius, was anointed with the Holy Spirit and with power (Acts 10:38); and when Jesus spoke of the gift of the Spirit which he was about to pass on to his disciples, it was sufficient for him to say that they would be clothed with power from on high (24:49). That the apostles did in fact receive Jesus' prophetical power and were therefore able, like him, to do mighty acts of healing and signs among the people, we shall see later on. From weak, frightened men they became giants in the apostolate, awe-inspiring in the strength and clarity of their purpose. They had received the strength of Christ. We so easily forget or pass quickly over the fierce intolerance and dominating power of Jesus. It was similar to that associated with the prophets of old, power at one and the same time over the body and the soul. Damning in his condemnation of pharisee and lawyer, irresistible in miracle and spiritual healing, it is Jesus' forcefulness, his dynamism and his demand for a total commitment which recall the preaching of past prophets and at the same time suggest something entirely new: here is an absoluteness of claim and of capacity explicable only if God himself is now present in the flesh. God in truth has become a prophet, fulfilling and reshaping both the old function of prophet and the old idea of God. Old things pass, and at the centre of the new testament is 'Jesus of Nazareth, a prophet powerful in word and act' (προφήτης δυνατὸς ἐν ἔργῳ καὶ λόγῳ, 24:19).

Jesus resembled his predecessors. I have spoken already of his likeness to the Servant of the Lord of Isaias, and must turn now to the resemblance with the two greatest historical prophets, Moses and Elias. When Jesus took Peter and John and James with him and went up the mountain and was transfigured before them, it was Moses and Elias who appeared and spoke with him. Jesus had already followed their example in his fast of forty days,[1] and now they came back to converse with him; the significance of this has been variously interpreted. For some, Moses stands for the Law and Elias for the prophets, so that together they represent the whole Old Testament doing homage in Jesus to the New. For others, Moses represents the dead, Elias (who never died) the living, and hence together they again constitute a wholeness of witness to Jesus. Without denying these interpretations, we may see the truer and deeper sense of their presence in their common prophetic character, and especially their closeness to God. They stand for the same rather than for different aspects of experience. These were the two men who had seen God on Horeb, and their presence adds meaning to the experience of the apostles who now on a mountain see the glory of Jesus and hear the voice of the Father; it also makes of Moses and Elias particularly reliable witnesses to Jesus, who is revealed not only as God but also as their successor, and especially as the prophet 'like unto me' foretold by Moses in Deuteronomy. Of this prophet Moses had said 'It is to him thou must listen', and on the mountain of the Transfiguration, as the figures of Moses and Elias disappear into the cloud, the voice of the Father is heard proclaiming 'This is my beloved Son; to him, then, listen' (9:35). The command is renewed, the prophet like unto Moses is identified.[2] St Stephen developed this in his long speech before the

[1] Deut. 9:9; 3 Kings 19:8.
[2] For the linking up of the Transfiguration text with Deuteronomy 18 see Dodd, *According to the Scriptures*, pp. 55–6.

Council, the chief point of that whole discourse being that it was because Jesus was the prophet like Moses foretold in Deuteronomy that he could be, like Moses, both rejected by Israel and at the same time Israel's true ruler and deliverer (Acts 7).[1]

It cannot be said that elsewhere Luke lays explicit stress on Jesus' resemblance to Moses. Explicit, I say, because his gospel certainly has Deuteronomy for one of its Old Testament foundations. The order of the events and discourses in his central section has always presented a great problem, because it is very difficult to see what order there is at all. The answer, it has been recently suggested,[2] lies in the order of Deuteronomy: St Luke followed its sequence in arranging his matter, so as to compose a sort of Christian Deuteronomy. In itself this does not seem to me an unlikely suggestion, yet the arguments fail to convince; and I see the danger of reading into slight similarities of order much more than is in fact there. But apart from the actual order of paragraphs, it seems very clear that the third gospel—and especially its central section—is in some ways closely related to Deuteronomy, and that through this Luke again suggests Jesus' character of a new Moses. Deuteronomy

[1] The point of St Stephen's reference to Deuteronomy 18 is clear enough; but that of St Peter in Acts 3:22 is less easy to understand. It appears to have been suggested by the word 'raise up'—the Greek verb ἀνίστημι—which comes in the oracle: The Lord God will raise up for you a prophet like myself. The same word being used in Greek for 'raise up' from the dead, Deuteronomy 18 became a prophecy of the Resurrection. St Peter's argument was based on the Greek Septuagint of Deuteronomy and does not hold with the original Hebrew. See Dom Jacques Dupont, *L'Utilisation Apologétique de l'Ancien Testament dans Les Discours des Actes* (Louvain, 1953).

[2] By C. F. Evans, 'The Central Section of St Luke's Gospel', *Studies in the Gospels* (Blackwell, 1955), pp. 37–54; and by Dr Farrer on pp. 77–9 of the same work.

is a very beautiful book, full not only of the law, but of the law's spirit, of the love and mercy of God which have inspired the law. Passages like chapter 30 may remind one of the third gospel, the gospel of mercy. The spirit of Deuteronomy must most certainly have appealed to Luke.

At the moment of the Transfiguration, when Jesus is revealed as the new Moses, he is in a similar position to Moses at the beginning of Deuteronomy. The Israel of Moses is about to leave Mount Horeb and to take possession of the promised land (Deut. 1:6–8), so Jesus coming down from the mountain was about to set off on his all-important journey to Jerusalem. But if Jesus is the prophet whose relation to Israel is like that of Moses (Deut. 18:15), the effect of his teaching is to be very different. The central law of the Deuteronomic code is that of the sanctuary (Deut. 12), the divine consecration of Jerusalem; but the life of Jesus was to culminate in the divine rejection of Jerusalem, and St Luke's gospel is the gospel of that rejection. Again, Deuteronomy calls for the destruction of the non-Jew nations (Deut. 7) and the sentence 'When the Lord thy God shall have destroyed the nations' is almost a refrain running through the book[1]; but St Luke is the evangelist of the calling of the nations, of the universal extension of that divine mercy, which the Deuteronomist had so well experienced within the fold of Israel. Jesus, the new Moses giving the new Deuteronomy, embraces much of the spirit of the old, but yet turns its whole construction upside down; and it is St Luke who most clearly illustrates the point.

But even more evidently Jesus in the third gospel is depicted as the new Elias.[2] 3 Kings 17 to 4 Kings 5 is another of

[1] Deut. 7:1; 11:23; 12:29; 19:1.

[2] Consult P. Dabeck, S.V.D., 'Siehe, Es Erschienen Moses und Elias',

the Old Testament foundations of St Luke's work. This is probably why Luke, to avoid confusion, omitted explicit references to the Elias character of John the Baptist. At the very opening of his public prophetic ministry at Nazareth Jesus compares himself with Elias:

> He said to them, No doubt you will tell me, as the proverb says, Physician, heal thyself; do here in thy own country all that we have heard of thy doing at Capharnaum. And he said, Believe me, no prophet finds acceptance in his own country. Why, you may be sure of this, there were many widows among the people of Israel in the days of Elias, when a great famine came over the land, after the heavens had remained shut for three years and six months, but Elias was not sent to any of these. He was sent to a widow in Sarepta, which belongs to Sidon (4:23-6).

This at once links up with Luke's account of the raising of the son of the widow of Naim (7:11-16) in which the similarity with Elias stands out clearly and prepares the way for the conclusion, 'A great prophet has risen up among us; God has visited his people.' But what is immediately and equally noticeable is the difference between Jesus and Elias. Jesus raises the son of the widow of Naim with a word; Elias brings back to life the son of the widow of Sarepta only after much prayer and lying on the corpse. Such little points suggest something of the transcendence over the old Elias—imposing figure though

---

Biblica, XXIII (1942), pp. 175-89. St Augustine calls Our Lord the 'True Elias' in sermon 201. St Caesarius of Arles develops the theme 'Beatus Elias typum habuit Domini' in his sermon 124. The idea is common to the Latin Fathers, and also to the Syrian Aphraates, but not it seems to the Greeks; cf. the three patristic studies in *Elie Le Prophète*, I: G. Bardy, 'Le Souvenir d'Elie chez les Pères Grecs' (pp. 131-58), M. Hayek, 'Elie dans la Tradition Syriaque' (pp. 159-77), and P. Hervé de l'Incarnation, O.C.D., 'Elie chez les Pères Latins' (pp. 179-207).

he was—of the new: of that tranquil plenitude of spiritual power which belonged to Jesus.

There can be no doubt that one of the key verses for the understanding of the third gospel, a verse to which we shall be constantly returning, is 9:51: 'And now the time was drawing near for his taking away from the earth, and he set his face steadfastly towards the way that led to Jerusalem.' It is the beginning of a new part of the book, the narrative of the journey to Jerusalem, and is a verse full of mystery and suggestiveness; there is more than a hint in it of the Elias theme, for Luke must surely have been thinking of 4 Kings 2:1, 'And now the time had come when the Lord would have Elias carried up by a whirlwind into heaven.' A last journey leading up to a solemn ascension is indicated in one and the other text; but while Elias was carried up into heaven in a fiery chariot and a whirlwind, Jesus was carried up quietly in a cloud.[1]

Immediately following this verse Luke narrates an incident which goes yet further to establish the parallel between Jesus and Elias. Jesus, he writes,

> sent messengers before him, who came into a Samaritan village, to make all in readiness. But the Samaritans refused to receive him, because his journey was in the direction of Jerusalem. When they found this, two of his disciples, James and John, asked him, Lord, wouldst thou have us bid fire come down from heaven and consume them? But he turned and rebuked them, You do not understand, he said, what spirit it is you share. The Son of Man has come to save men's lives, not to destroy them. And so they passed on to another village (9:52–6).[2]

[1] Compare 4 Kings 2:11 with Lk. 24:51; Acts 1:9–10.

[2] This text is that of the Vulgate. Many of the best Greek manuscripts, including Vaticanus and Sinaiticus, have a shorter text ending 'But he turned and rebuked them. And so they passed on to another village.' However

Elias had been the great bringer of fire to the earth—physical, material fire, able to consume men and offerings,[1] and the apostles had understood Jesus' mission as the new Elias, but not its true spiritual and interior character, the elevation of Elias' fiery activity on to an entirely new plane. For the fire which Jesus had come to bring was of another kind, one which does not destroy but saves, the very fire of the Holy Spirit. He had come, as John the Baptist had already said, to baptize 'with the Holy Spirit and with fire'[2] (3:16) and this baptism was to be offered to the whole world: 'It is fire that I have come to spread over the earth [not just over one little Samaritan village], and what do I desire but that it should be kindled' (12:49). It was to be kindled at Pentecost, when tongues of fire came down on the Apostles and they were all filled with the Holy Spirit (Acts 2:3–4), and its spreading over the earth is the theme of Luke's second book, the *Acts*. Not only the Ascension but also Pentecost manifests Jesus as a new Elias, especially as this passing on of Jesus' spirit to his disciples after they had seen him go up to heaven is reminiscent of the passing

another large group of manuscripts, including the Koridethi codex of the 'Caesarean' family of manuscripts, and above all the Codex Bezae, chief representative of the 'Western' text, give not only the full text as found in the Vulgate but also add to the Apostles' question the words 'as Elias did'. It has been suggested that both these additions are due to Marcion, but that is not in the least proved; they may well be older than that. Whether or not they are authentically Lucan, they seem in perfect accord with the mind of Luke.

[1] 4 Kings 1:10–12; 3 Kings 18:36–8.

[2] For John the Baptist fire was the image not of the Holy Spirit of God but of the approaching divine judgment. He was speaking of the messianic judgment which would definitively sanctify God's people. Cf. P. Van Imschoot, 'Baptême d'Eau et Baptême d'Esprit Saint', *Ephemerides Theologicae Lovanienses* (1936), pp. 653–66. But it can hardly be doubted that for Luke the fire to which John referred was already a symbol of the Holy Spirit, as it has been ever since.

on of Elias' spirit to Eliseus. In both cases this passing on of the Spirit enabled the disciple to perform the mighty works of his master: Eliseus raised up the dead son of the Sunamitess, St Peter Tabitha—both women abounding in charity and alms-deeds.[1] Both miracles are followed by the intervention and conversion of Gentiles: Naaman in one case, Cornelius in the other, both foreign officers.[2] The parallels are remarkable and would seem to be deliberate.

A few lines further on in chapter nine of the third gospel is a strange verse, which again requires for its understanding a comparison with the story of Elias. 'And there was yet another who said, Lord, I will follow thee, but first let me take leave of my friends. To him Jesus said, No one who looks behind him, when he has once put his hand to the plough, is fitted for the kingdom of God' (9:61–2). At once we think of Elias and his disciple Eliseus, who was permitted to take leave of his father and mother before following his master (3 Kings 19: 19–21). Jesus' call has an absoluteness which exceeds that of the old prophet, just as his work has a truly spiritual character very different from that of the extraordinary miracles which filled the life of his predecessor. The new Elias possesses the characteristics of the historical Elias, but in a transcendentally original way.

I may now summarize St Luke's contribution to this subject. The earliest Christian writers, following Our Lord himself, certainly saw Jesus as the great prophet of Deuteronomy, the New Moses. Jesus had instituted a new covenant, a new law, and Moses was his obvious predecessor. Elias was not: his importance was not as predecessor but as precursor of the

[1] 4 Kings 4:8–37; Acts 9:36–43.
[2] 4 Kings 5:1–15; Acts 10:1–48.

Messiah,[1] and his mission was understood as fulfilled in John the Baptist's preaching. St Luke, either deliberately or inadvertently, restated the nature of this relationship. In his gospel Elias appears less as precursor than as another predecessor, almost more important than Moses himself. Our Lord, not John, becomes the New Elias, and explicit references to the Baptist as Elias are almost eliminated. Elias' prayer and fasts foreshadow those of Jesus, and his bringing down of fire Jesus' gift of the Spirit; Elias' dwelling with the widow of Sarepta prefigures the mission to the Gentiles[2]; finally Elias' departure from the earth is the type of Jesus' Ascension. 3 Kings 17—4 Kings 5 is, I conclude, a most important foundation for St Luke's work, in particular for his ninth gospel chapter.

[1] This idea of Moses being predecessor, Elias precursor, I owe to Dr Ramsey, *The Glory of God and the Transfiguration of Christ*, p. 114; he in turn owes it to J. Jeremias, *Theologisches Wörterbuch* II, 930–43.

[2] As we shall see better in chapter six, when I speak of Jesus' visit to Nazareth. This piece of typology became a Western patristic commonplace: 'For St Augustine, St Gregory, St Caesarius, St Isidore, the career of Elias prefigures the future rejection of the Jews and the calling of the pagans' (P. Hervé de l'Incarnation, O.C.D., in *Elie Le Prophète*, I, pp. 202–3).

JESUS PRAYING, THE HOLY SPIRIT CAME
DOWN UPON HIM

In the biblical perspective the Holy Spirit and the gift of prophecy go together, one follows on from the other. The Rabbis habitually called the Spirit of God the 'Spirit of prophecy', and when in post-exilic Israel there were no more prophets they felt that the Spirit too had been withdrawn from the nation: 'Since the death of Aggaeus, Zacharias and Malachy, who are the last prophets,' they wrote,[1] 'the Holy Spirit has been no more in Israel.' Hence it is not surprising, given his interest in prophecy, that the Holy Spirit too has a special importance for St Luke, and that his writings have even been called 'the gospel of the Holy Ghost'. The Spirit is certainly referred to more frequently in the third than in the other gospels, while the Acts are a veritable chronicle of His activities.

Another title the third gospel has received is 'the gospel of prayer', and here again there is to be found an unmistakable stress: 'He would steal away from them into the desert and pray there' (5:16) Luke remarks of Our Lord, summing up

[1] Tsota, XIII, 2; quoted by J. Giblet in *L'Attente du Messie*, p. 93.

an aspect of Jesus' life which he places in special relief. These two ideas need to be studied together; moreover they only take on their full significance in the light of the previous chapter's theme—Jesus' character of prophet. It was as a prophet that Jesus was led by the Spirit, as a prophet that he entered the desert or went up the mountain to pray like Moses or Elias, the great men of prayer of the past.[1]

When speaking of the Holy Spirit St Luke follows closely in the Old Testament tradition; this is particularly evident in the first chapters of both his books which are so near the pre-Christian dispensation. The word 'Spirit' originally meant a strong breath or wind, to be contrasted with the flabby flesh that is man and created things generally. In the Old Testament the Spirit was not recognized as a distinct divine person, but rather the power of God acting in the world, guiding his people, going before them in the column of fire through the desert, present to the individual as to the nation, and indeed to the whole of things, over which in their primeval condition of un-formed waters he had creatively moved. It was only after Pentecost that in the fruitful play of the young Church's experience the Spirit was really known and appreciated as a distinct person and constant comforter, and the teaching of Jesus on this score fully understood. But already in the Old Testament there had been progress and purification, going from an early and quasi-physical notion of wind to the Spirit who is called holy in a poem of Isaias (63:10, 11). This progress was most clearly marked in the matter of prophetic inspiration. It was always through the action of the Spirit of God that someone became a prophet or representative of God;

[1] For the prayer of Moses and Elias, cf. Ex. 17:11; 32:11; Ps. 105:23; 3 Kings 17:1; 18:36–46; James 5:17–18.

but at first the idea of inspiration was a very material one. For example, in the book of Judges the descent of the Lord's Spirit could make a man a great soldier, full of tough strength, like Samson who was bound by the Philistines with two new ropes and carried off a prisoner;

> Loud was the Philistines' cry of triumph that went up to meet him at Lechi; but suddenly the spirit of the Lord came upon him, and his bonds parted and snapped like scorched tow. No weapon had he, but he found a bone lying there, an ass's jaw-bone; took that instead, and killed a thousand men with it. With the bone of an ass, he cried, I have made bones of them; with the bone of an ass a thousand men lie slain (Jud. 15:14–16).

From a war-leader we may turn to a group of ecstatics, musicians or religious revivalists. After anointing the young Saul, Samuel told him

> Thou wilt come to the Hill of God, where the Philistines have set a garrison; and here, upon entering the city, thou wilt meet a company of prophets coming down from the sacred height. With harp and tambour, flute and zither at their head, they will be uttering words of prophecy; and with that the spirit of the Lord will fall upon thee, making thee prophesy with the rest, and turning thee into a new man (1 Sam. 10:5–6).

A company of prophets of this type seems to have been especially attached to a shrine ('the sacred height'), and their work was connected with the cult and worship of God which was there carried out. The rather strange situation that could develop when the spirit of the Lord fell on someone, on this occasion again Saul and his men, is well described in 1 Samuel 19:19–24.

These texts suggest what the primitive Israelite idea of prophetic inspiration was like. In those early times there was much more interest in the form than the content of prophecy, in the visible accidentals rather than the lasting meaning of a divine revelation. We must not underrate such great early prophetic figures as Samuel, Elias and Eliseus, but by and large there was little harmony between the spirit and the flesh, and no transformation of flesh by spirit, but a mere transient taking of possession[1]; this is especially true as a prophet could be temperamentally suited to his mission and yet of most immoral character.[2] Many of those of the company type were clearly not supernatural prophets at all but regular members of a possibly not unlucrative profession, and they may have owed their origin much more to surviving Canaanite religion than to that of the Israelites. Anyway the frequent wildness and immorality of these men gave them a bad name, and so we find that those later and immeasurably greater prophets who begin with Amos were very reluctant to use the name at all or to speak of themselves as inspired, even if some of them may have originally belonged to a cultic prophet association of the old kind. It is this situation which explains the round condemnations of men like Michaeas: 'This message the Lord has for prophets that guide my people amiss, prophets that must have their mouths filled ere they will cry, All's well! Sop thou must give them, else thou shalt be their sworn enemy. Visions would you see, all shall be night around you, search you the skies, you shall search in the dark; never a prophet but his sun is set, his day turned into twilight' (Mich. 3 : 5–6). Whatever the previous occupation of true prophets may have been, they owe their

---

[1] See the remarks of Fr Richard Kehoe, O.P., *The Holy Spirit in the Scriptures*, Selection II (ed. C. Hastings and D. Nicholl) (Sheed & Ward, 1954), pp. 2–4.

[2] Cf. St Thomas' judgment in the *De Veritate*, XII. Good morals are not needed for prophecy (5 ad 6), but a good imagination is (4 ad 2).

powers entirely to a special divine vocation, and did not wish to be taken for professional diviners: 'What, said Amos, I a prophet? Nay, not that, nor a prophet's son neither[1]; I am one that minds cattle, one that nips the sycamore-trees; I was but tending sheep when the Lord took me into his service. It was the Lord bade me go and prophesy to his people of Israel' (Amos 7:14–15).

Yet the name of prophet remained in use among the true prophets as the last passage shows; there was no alternative; and somewhat chary as they were of speaking of their inspired character (Ezechiel was not), they were well aware of what they were and that the Spirit of God was the source of their prophecy.[2] In Deutero-Isaias' ideal figure of the Servant of the Lord, who was certainly a prophet, the Spirit's presence is clearly indicated. But the concrete conception of prophecy was changing, becoming more interior, more concerned with the message with its source and significance, and less with the technical phenomena. For the Spirit was no longer just taking possession, but was beginning to transform humanity. Its action remained violent and unpredictable, but this violence was now not so much in the physical as in the moral order; while the revelation afforded was such as to transform the very dimensions of the religion of Israel. The Spirit was truly entering into man. The historical movement in the action of the Spirit and the gift of prophecy was from the external to the internal, and its Old Testament culmination may be found in the figures of Jeremias and the suffering servant of Isaias.

[1] According to H. H. Rowley what Amos said was 'I *was* no prophet or son of a prophet', see *The Old Testament and Modern Study*, p. 142. He became a prophet when called by the Lord.

[2] They tended to speak more of their revelation as coming from the Word than from the Spirit of God.

However, Jeremias is a type and the suffering servant a prophecy of one still to come, for the real enduring gift and seal of the Spirit had not yet been given. Only in the prophet Jesus is it found. His fullness of the Spirit is a new thing, deeper, quieter, more effective. There is no straining to make use of the Spirit's power; he has it at all times from the moment of his conception. At last humanity, flesh, is fully transformed by the Spirit of God, and the movement of prophetic progress has reached its term. Moreover when we thus see Jesus as the Spirit-filled man, successor to the prophets of the past, we are not denying his divine nature or suggesting some doctrine of subordination; no, we are remaining faithful to the scriptural witness, and we are further entering a little into the true relationship of the Old and the New Testaments. As Fr Victor White has illuminatingly remarked, 'The New Testament is not merely a fulfilment of the context of the Old, it is a fulfilment of its *mode*. No longer does the Word of God merely *use* human flesh, . . . he *becomes* it.'[1] No longer does he merely use human prophets, he becomes himself a prophet. If we search the fact of Jesus' prophetical union with the Spirit to obtain its full meaning, we arrive at nothing short of his divinity. For his fullness of the Spirit is no longer a being possessed but a possessing. The Spirit of God is the Spirit of Jesus, and Jesus is not only led by the Spirit but also sends him. Man can be led by the Spirit, but a man who can send and so command the Spirit of God—or who can baptize with the Spirit—can be no other than God made man. The theology of Jesus prophet covers in its own way the whole sweep of Christology from the heights of the divinity to the depths of the suffering servant.

In the tradition of Israel the gift of the Spirit was connected

[1] *God and the Unconscious*, pp. 134–5.

6

not only with the vocation of the prophet but also with that of the Messiah who was to come. In the thought of Isaias, Emmanuel, the coming Messiah, was to be filled with the Spirit: 'The Spirit of the Lord shall rest upon him: the spirit of wisdom and of understanding, the spirit of counsel and of fortitude, the spirit of knowledge and of the fear of the Lord' (Is. 11:1–2). And in the first song of the servant of the Lord, which—as we have seen—may have already been understood messianically in pre-Christian times, it is said that he has been clothed with the Spirit (Is. 42:1). Though not much is said in the Old Testament about the Spirit anointing of the Messiah, the gap is made up to some extent by other Jewish writings of the time just before and after Our Lord: thus we read among the Zadokite fragments (2:10), probably of the first century A.D., that 'through his Messiah he shall make them know his Holy Spirit'.[1] On the whole, Old Testament thinking was concerned more with messianic times and the messianic community than with the person of the Messiah himself. We may think of the famous passage of the prophet Joel which St Peter saw as fulfilled at Pentecost: 'I will pour out my spirit upon all mankind, and your sons and daughters will be prophets. Your old men shall dream dreams, and your young men see visions; everywhere servants of mine, handmaids of mine, inspired to prophesy!' (Joel 2:28–9). This means that the messianic time was to witness a quite unprecedented outpouring of spiritual gifts upon the messianic community, *a fortiori* upon its head. In those circles where a prophet-messiah was expected, this was even more stressed, as the Spirit remained supremely the Spirit of prophecy. It was

[1] For this and other texts see Barrett, *The Holy Spirit and the Gospel Tradition*, pp. 42–4.

especially to such circles that the little work utilized by St Luke in his first gospel chapters would have appealed.

The great majority of references to the Holy Spirit in the third gospel are in these first chapters. The aim is clear. After so many dry years the Spirit has returned to Israel and in a way never before experienced, in a very flood of prophecy. The conclusion was obvious: the prophet-messiah had come. We have already considered the first prophet to appear in the gospel story, John the Baptist, who 'from the time when he is yet a child in his mother's womb shall be filled with the Holy Ghost' (1:15). But it was not only John who received the Spirit in this anticipation of the outpouring of Pentecost. He descended upon all those connected with the earth-coming of Jesus— upon Mary, Elizabeth, Zachary and Simeon. And each, as he or she was filled by the Spirit, cried out in a prophecy of exultation, for some part of the long-awaited mystery of redemption had just been revealed. The aged Simeon was waiting patiently for the consolation of Israel:

> The Holy Spirit was upon him: and by the Holy Spirit it had been revealed to him that he was not to meet death, until he had seen that Christ whom the Lord had anointed. He now came, led by the Spirit, into the temple; and when the child Jesus was brought in by his parents, to perform the custom which the law enjoined concerning him, Simeon too was able to take him in his arms (2:26–28).

Simeon was joined by Anna, an ancient prophetess; and though these two old people were probably not of much worldly importance in Jerusalem, they were seen by Christians as representatives of the old order inspired to recognize the new. The effect in every case of the Spirit's action is the same: prayer and thanksgiving to God. What are the *Benedictus*, the

Magnificat, the *Nunc Dimittis* but the most splendid of inspired prayers? And Anna too, we are told, though her words are not recorded, 'came near to give God thanks' (2:38).

If the friends and relatives all shared in the good gift of God at Jesus' coming, it was of course Jesus himself who was the chief recipient of the Holy Spirit. The power of the Spirit was upon him not only in his mother's womb, like John, but already in his very conception (1:35). Luke wants to say that the whole of Jesus' life was supernatural, that his prophetic character was not only functional, the effect of a vocation given to one already existing, but ontological; he was prophet through and through from the first instant. This hidden prophetic and messianic character is revealed in the Jordan at the moment of his baptism, when the Spirit descends upon him in bodily form as a dove and the voice of the Father is heard from heaven saying 'Thou art my beloved Son, in thee I am well pleased' (3:22). These words and the descent of the Spirit are the clearest reference to Isaias 42:1: 'Behold my servant: I will uphold him, My elect: my soul delighteth in him. I have given my spirit upon him; he shall bring forth judgment to the Gentiles.' At one and the same moment Jesus is revealed as the Servant of the Lord, Messiah, and Son of God. The coming and manifestation of the Messiah inaugurates a new age, a new Israel, indeed a new creation. That is why Luke takes Jesus' genealogy back to Adam, and not only, like Matthew, to Abraham. Jesus' baptism in the Jordan echoes the first lines of Genesis; as the creative Spirit moved over the waters out of which came the first earth, so now the Spirit descends on the head of the new creation as he comes up out of the waters of Jordan.[1]

[1] But the baptism itself had less importance for Luke than it had for Matthew

It is interesting for a moment to consider the relation for Luke between Jesus' titles of Messiah (Christ) and Son of God. It would be wrong to separate them too much and consider the first as merely functional and redemptive, the second as purely ontological and divine. There is, of course, no possible doubt that Luke, friend and companion of Paul, believed in Jesus' divinity, believed that Jesus was in the most absolute sense the unique Son of God. Yet this title was also for him genuinely messianic; the two in fact go together, and they are linked especially by the Spirit's action. 'The Holy Spirit will come upon thee, and the power of the most High will over-shadow thee. Thus this holy offspring of thine shall be known for the Son of God' (1:35). Again at Jesus' messianic baptism the descent of the Spirit coincides with the Father's words 'Thou art my beloved Son'. If it is as prophet-messiah that he receives the Spirit, he receives it also because he is the Son of God. Whereas in the first gospel Peter confessed that Jesus was 'the Christ, the Son of the living God' (Mt. 16:16), Luke, following Mark, simply gives 'Thou art the Christ whom God has anointed' (9:20), anointed surely with the Spirit in the Jordan; and the difference between the two accounts should not be over-stressed. At Jesus' trial, however, the two titles seem clearly distinguished in St Luke's gospel, the first question of the chief priest 'If thou art the Christ, tell us' is followed by a second, 'Thou art, then, the Son of God?' (22:66, 70) and it was Jesus' reply to this that proved his blasphemy. Only Luke separates the questions in this way and it shows a desire to stress, here at the end of his gospel, Jesus' claim to be Son

and Mark—it is disposed of in a subordinate clause. For him the significant fact was the descent of the Spirit. This tendency was continued in John where the baptism is not mentioned at all (Jn. 1:32–3).

of God not merely as Messiah but beyond this by intimate right of his very nature—his messiahship was evidence of his sonship but did not exhaust it. He died because he claimed to be God.

But we must return to the threshold of the public life. 'Jesus returned from the Jordan, full of the Holy Spirit, and by the Spirit he was led on into the wilderness where he remained forty days, tempted by the devil' (4:1-2). Here again the Spirit is not leading him on for his own sake, but because he is the Messiah. His temptations are messianic: they are the temptations of the false worldly nationalist messianism of the Jews of that time, and moreover they are temptations akin to those which Israel had felt and succumbed to in the forty years in the desert; hence in each temptation Jesus replies to the devil with words chosen from Deuteronomy. The first temptation, that of bread, is comparable with Israel's temptation described in Numbers 11:33-4; and Jesus replies to it with the text of Deuteronomy 8:3. The second (following Luke's order), that of the high mountain, should be compared with Exodus 32; Jesus answers with Deuteronomy 6:13. His third temptation, that of the temple, is similar to Israel's narrated in Exodus 17:1-7, and he rejects it with Deuteronomy 6:16. His forty days are in fact the renewal of Israel's forty years[1]; both were led by the Spirit, but where Israel had failed Jesus triumphed, and so could fittingly enter into the kingdom and his messianic ministry.

He came back to Galilee, we are told, with the power of the Spirit upon him, and entering the synagogue at Nazareth on the Sabbath day he began to read from the sixty-first chapter of

[1] See J. Guillet's treatment of the Exodus theme in *Thèmes Bibliques* (Aubier, 1950), pp. 9-25.

Isaias: 'The Spirit of the Lord is upon me; he has anointed me, and sent me out to preach the gospel to the poor . . . to proclaim a year when men may find acceptance with the Lord' (4:18–19). This was to say that he was beginning his ministry as prophet and Messiah anointed by the Spirit, as the servant of the Lord foretold by Isaias; and it sets the tone for the whole ministry.

After this there are far fewer references to the Spirit in the third gospel; and indeed there is no need for them. Some are unnecessarily worried about the comparative lack of references to the Holy Ghost in the gospels—and especially in Jesus' own recorded words—in comparison with the Acts and the Epistles. Incidentally that lack is very good evidence of the gospels' historical value; in spite of the early Christians' tremendous Spirit-consciousness, they resisted the temptation to fill up their accounts of Jesus' teaching with references to the Spirit. But all the gospels are in agreement that Jesus' human career was inaugurated by the Spirit's messianic anointing and all agree that Jesus promised his disciples the help of the Spirit in future difficulties. There was no need for more, prior to Jesus' final instructions about the gift the disciples were shortly to receive.

Nevertheless throughout the third gospel we find a considerable number of references to the Holy Spirit, many of which are doubtless due to the preoccupations of its author. A good number are linked with the prayer of Jesus, and it is this theme of the Spirit and prayer which we must now consider, starting with that first most mysterious moment when Jesus appeared at the Jordan where John was baptizing. 'It was while all the people were being baptized that Jesus was baptized too, and stood there praying. Suddenly heaven was

opened, and the Holy Spirit came down upon him in bodily
form' (3:21–2). It was 'Jesus praying' who was thus initially
anointed by the Spirit, and though every subsequent reference
by Luke to Jesus' prayer is not connected with a reference to
the Spirit, nor vice versa, yet there is a certain harmony
between the two which it is not difficult to feel.

In chapter 10 we find the very words of one of Our Lord's
prayers, that concerning the Father's revelation to the little
ones: 'At this time, Jesus was filled with gladness by the Holy
Spirit and said, O Father, who art Lord of heaven and earth,
I give thee praise that thou hast hidden all this from the wise
and the prudent, and revealed it to little children. Be it so,
Lord, since this finds favour in thy sight' (10:21). Matthew
gives the same prayer (Mt. 11:25–7) but not the opening
phrase, which is St Luke's own, and characteristic in bringing
together three of his favourite ideas: gladness, prayer, the Holy
Spirit. It is when in prayer that Jesus is closest to the Holy
Spirit, but also of course to his Father. At such times, leaving
aside his disciples, he remains alone united with God. His are
not primarily prayers of petition, but simply of union, of that
mutual exchange of love which he does not find with men.
Among men he teaches, he cures, he is the master, but he is
alone; only when solitary in prayer does he cease to be a solitary in entering into the society of his equals.[1] From this point
of view, far from being the most human, his prayer is rather the
most divine of all Jesus' activities; it is in it that he most truly
shows himself the equal of the Father, the Beloved Son, as in
those last most lovely prayers—'Father, forgive them; they
know not what they do' and 'Father, into thy hands I com-

[1] See the suggestive remarks of S. Garofalo, 'La Preghiera solitaria di
Gesù', *Euntes Docete* (1955), especially pp. 166–9.

mend my Spirit' (23:34, 46). But Jesus' prayer is also an integral part of his messianic mission: as the Spirit-guided
prophet-messiah he communicates with the Spirit above all in
his periods of prayer.

We must catch the rhythm of St Luke's references to the
prayer of Jesus. It is not just that he frequently mentions that
Our Lord prayed, more frequently than the other evangelists:
it is when he prayed that must be noted. Jesus' public ministry
opens with the prayer of the Jordan and closes with the prayer
of the Cross; and all the more important events between are
commenced in prayer. Let us consider them.

> It was at this time that he went out onto the mountain side, and
> passed the whole night offering prayer to God, and when day
> dawned, he called his disciples to him, choosing out twelve of
> them; these he called his apostles (6:12–13).
>
> There was a time when he had gone apart to pray, and his
> disciples were with him; and he asked them, who do the multi-
> tude say that I am? They answered John the Baptist; others say
> Elias, others that one of the old prophets has returned to life.
> Then he said to them, But who do you say that I am? And Peter
> answered, Thou art the Christ whom God has anointed (9:18–
> 20).
>
> It was about a week after all this was said, that he took Peter
> and John and James with him, and went up on to the mountain
> side to pray. And even as he prayed, the fashion of his face was
> altered, and his garments became white and dazzling (9:28–9).
>
> Once when he had found a place to pray in, one of his disciples
> said to him, after his prayer was over, Lord, teach us to pray, as
> John did for his disciples. And he told them, when you pray,
> you are to say, Father, . . . (11:1–2)

The choosing of the twelve; St Peter's act of faith at Caesarea; the Transfiguration; the teaching of the Lord's own

prayer: these are the most important single events in the public ministry as it appears in the Synoptics. It is Luke alone who links each of them with the prayer of Christ. Only he explicitly makes the prayer taught to the disciples a prolongation of Jesus' own—which it most truly was, for it began with the word 'Father'. Nothing incidentally could be more mistaken than the idea which makes the Lord's prayer just a beautiful expression of natural religion. It is, on the contrary, intrinsically Christian: a sharing in Christ's own prayer. Only Luke tells us that the choosing of the Twelve followed a night of prayer on the mountain side.[1] This last was a moment of great solemnity; Our Lord's long prayer must have concerned his future apostles, still so weak but needing to be so strong, men to whom everything that Jesus stood for was to be committed. Was it to this occasion that he was referring when later, on the night of the last supper, he declared 'Simon, Simon, . . . I have prayed for thee, that thy faith may not fail' (22:31–2)? And if he chose his apostles in prayer, did he not choose them through the Holy Spirit? Luke himself tells us that he did.[2] Chosen in prayer, through the Holy Spirit, they received from him, that their faith might not fail, that Spirit—'The Spirit of Jesus'— which he himself possessed.

I have already spoken more than once of that strange, un-public episode of the Transfiguration, which comes in the very middle of the public ministry, when Jesus and his three companions went up alone on to 'the holy mountain' (2 Pet. 1:18) and something of his divine glory was made manifest

---

[1] It was why the choosing of the supplementary member of the Twelve should also begin with prayer (Acts 1:24–5).

[2] Acts 1:2, as it is to be found in a well-supported variant reading. Cf. Larranaga, *L'Ascension de Notre Seigneur* (Rome, 1938), pp. 174–6.

to them. Never did he appear nearer to the Father. In this moment of intense prayer his glory is revealed as at once the beloved Son and the prophet like unto Moses to whom all must listen. As prophet and man of prayer, Jesus converses with those two great figures of prayer from the past, Moses and Elias; at the same time, as the Father's beloved son he is seen to transcend them wholly in his personal union with God.

From the glory of the mountain to the agony of the garden: the greatest of all Jesus' works was about to be accomplished, and hence

> He parted from them going a stone's throw off, and knelt down to pray; Father, he said, if it please thee, take away this chalice from before me; only as thy will is, not as mine is. And he had sight of an angel from heaven, encouraging him. And now he was in an agony, and prayed still more earnestly; his sweat fell to the ground like thick drops of blood (22:41-4).

Whenever we find Jesus in prayer we enter into the realms of mystery, whether the mood be gladness, glory or agony. What theological problems are raised! Luke does not try to resolve them; he is content to present Jesus as he sees him. Being fully man, Our Lord could be fully a prophet, could be filled by the Spirit, could be encouraged by an angel, could feel all the need and the anguish of prayer; but being the Son of God, Jesus could be fully divine, could send the Spirit, could be transfigured on the mountain, could talk as an equal with his Father.

The presence of the Spirit was to be a characteristic not only of the Messiah but also of the new messianic community—the Christian Church. Jesus had already promised his followers this gift when he told them, 'When they bring you to trial before synagogues, and magistrates, and officers, do not consider anxiously what you are to say, what defence to make or how to make it; the Holy Spirit will instruct you when the time comes, what words to use' (12:11–12). But it was after the Resurrection that, according to Luke, he told them of the general gift of the Spirit which they were soon to receive: 'I am sending down upon you the gift which was promised by my Father' (24:49 and Acts 1:8). This was the baptism with the Spirit which John had prophesied long before, and which would otherwise have had no meaning. With these last words of Jesus preceding his Ascension, which recall the words of the Precursor at the opening of the public ministry, we pass from Jesus to the Church, from the prophet-messiah to the community he left behind him. The fullness of the Spirit remains, such a fullness as permitted the disciples at Jerusalem to write that most astonishing sentence, 'It hath seemed good to the Holy Spirit and to us' (Acts 15:28). This continuity of the Spirit's presence is brought out by the parallelism between Luke's two books; as the Spirit had descended on Jesus in the Jordan he now descends upon Jesus' disciples in the upper room, and each is the opening of a ministry.

The close connection between the Holy Spirit and prophecy to be found in the Old Testament and also in Luke's account of Christ is much less evident in the New Testament as a whole. The realities remained but were transformed according to the requirements of a new situation. The primordial fact of the Church's life was indeed the abiding gift of the same Spirit which had moved the prophets and filled the Lord, and it took Christians some time to realize that this gift would take various forms in their new and more diversified religious economy. On receiving the Spirit at Pentecost it was natural for Peter to conclude that the apostles were now all prophets (Acts 2:14–20), which of course they were, as they had been introduced into the mystery of 'God's fixed design and fore-knowledge' (Acts 2:23), and a distinction between apostle and prophet[1] only gradually emerged; yet it was the very institution of apostles, and of the apostolic succession (this latter already evident in the choice of Matthias, Acts 1:15–26) which had radically changed the position of the prophet in the new dispensation.

The name 'apostle' means 'sent forth' and this at once shows a link between the new and the old, for the prophets were those who were 'sent', and Jesus of all prophets was most clearly 'the sent one'; hence also the title of 'apostle' became him as no other, and was given to him by the author of Hebrews (3:1). But the sending of his apostles was different from that of the prophets. It was definitive and consequently transcended the personal vocation of the one chosen, in that this new 'sending' was transmissible. The apostolic succession is an altogether different thing from a succession of prophets. No longer is the gift granted each time anew from above, it is passed on within the organism of a self-renewing group. Only little by little did the first Christians realize that they had out-lived the old type of prophetical economy, and that there were new activities, equally Spirit-governed, but called now by other names than prophecy—witnessing, for example, the primary activity of an apostle. Prophecy *eo nomine* remained, to be sure, a valued gift of the Holy Spirit, and a natural sequence to the laying on of hands (Acts 19:6); while prophets like Agabus[2] clearly fulfilled an important function in Christian

[1] 1 Cor. 12:29; Eph. 4:11.
[2] Acts 11:28; 21:10.

society. It was nevertheless a secondary function.[1] Instead, witnessing had become the most important of Spirit-guided activities in the New Testament. Hence the old identification of prophecy with the gift of the Spirit slowly disappeared; and Paul, so completely under the Spirit's guidance, was hardly given the title of prophet at all. The Spirit's action was seen as all-important in early Christian experience, and consequently not just one but all the varied activities of Christian life were regarded as his gifts and graces: 'There are different kinds of gifts, though it is the same Spirit who gives them' (1 Cor. 12:4). And behind the varied activities proper to different groups of Christians there was the common and supreme gift, that 'seal' which was and is imparted to each and every Christian and which is signified by the simple statement that he has received the Holy Spirit.[2] All the special gifts and charismas are only specializations of this primordial sanctification.

The Spirit was essentially for the first Christians the 'Spirit of Jesus' (Acts 16:7), and it was natural that its action should make them all like Jesus in other ways too. Christians, by the Spirit's power, not only witnessed to Jesus but shared his character. Thus they received that power (δύναμις) of his which was, as we know, especially a prophetical power and

[1] For the continuing function of prophets in the Church, cf. my essay 'The Prophet's rôle in the living Church', *Downside Review*, January 1956, pp. 38–47.

[2] It is not easy to know with what external rite the basic gift of the Holy Spirit was ordinarily associated. Cornelius and his people received the Spirit before baptism (Acts 10:44), but this was clearly exceptional. Baptism appears, as one would expect, to have been the normal vehicle of the gift (Acts 2:38), but we are explicitly told that the baptized Samaritans did not receive the Holy Spirit until the apostles laid hands on them (Acts 8:15–16). Baptism and the laying on of hands are clearly distinguished in Acts 19:5–6 and Hebrews 6:2.

of the Holy Spirit. Jesus promised it to them after the Resurrection with the gift of the Spirit, yet it was to make them not prophets, as one might at first have expected, but witnesses: 'You shall receive the power of the Holy Ghost coming upon you, and you shall be witnesses unto me in Jerusalem, and in all Judaea and Samaria, and even to the uttermost part of the earth' (Acts 1:8). This text is one of the keys to the whole of St Luke's work, as we shall see bit by bit. The prophets of the Old Testament were already witnesses to Christ (Acts 10:43), and so it is not surprising to find that the witness is the prophet of the New Testament; it is Jesus' prophetical power passed on through the Holy Ghost which makes his disciples witnesses (see also Acts 4:33), and enables them to perform the same mighty acts and signs which he had performed. The supreme opportunity for witnessing was in trial and persecution: for these occasions the Spirit's inspiration was especially promised (Lk. 12:11–12) and hence it is not surprising that it is precisely at these moments that the prophetic character of witnessing stands out clearest. 'They will lay their hands on you and persecute you, delivering you up to the synagogues and into prisons, dragging you before kings and governors, for my name's sake. That is your opportunity to give witness. Lay it up therefore in your hearts not to meditate before how you shall answer: For I will give you a mouth and wisdom, which all your adversaries shall not be able to resist and gainsay' (Lk. 21: 12–15). Recall the words of God to Moses, 'I will be in thy mouth: and I will teach thee what thou shalt speak' (Ex. 4:12) and the prophecy of Deuteronomy, 'I will raise them up a prophet out of the midst of their brethren like to thee. And I will put my words in his mouth: and he shall speak to them all that I shall command him. And he that will not hear the words

which he shall speak in my name, I will be the revenger'
(Deut. 18:18–19). It suggests that the prophecy of Deuteronomy is fulfilled not only in Jesus but also in the Christian
community which carries on his prophetic function precisely
through witnessing to him.[1]

Again, the Christian community was one of prayer, carrying
on the constant prayer of Jesus, according to his command
(Lk. 21:36), but like him praying above all at the decisive
moments of its life. Acts 4:23–31 beautifully and strikingly
unites these different characteristics which the Church in-
herited from her founder. John and Peter, set free by the chief
priests and elders, return to their people, and all together pray
to God a prayer whose wording is surely far earlier than Luke.
Recalling Psalm 2, 'said through thy Holy Spirit', and its fulfilment in the Passion of Jesus, the prayer continues, 'Look
down upon their threats, Lord, now as of old; enable thy
servants to preach thy word confidently, by stretching out thy
hand to heal; and let signs and miracles be performed in the
name of Jesus, thy holy Son.' After the prayer Luke tells us
'the place in which they had gathered rocked to and fro, and
they were all filled with the Holy Spirit, and began to preach
the word of God with confidence.' In this very early incident
(a sort of second Pentecost) the prophetical character of the
Christian community is very clearly marked. Later on it was
to be given less importance; but if the descent of the Spirit
ceased to be visibly manifest, it remained for all that equally
efficacious, while its effects became increasingly diversified.

It would obviously be quite wrong to think then that the
Old Testament connection between the Holy Spirit and prophecy soon ceased to exist or to have any meaning: on the

[1] The assimilation of witnessing with prophecy is made explicit in Apoc. 11.

contrary, prophecy had been, and in large part continued to be, the standard gift in terms of which others were understood; and the solemn act of witnessing—a Christian's highest duty and privilege—not only remained closely akin to prophesying, but was rightly regarded as an explicit continuation of the prophecy of the Old Testament. This is particularly clear in the transitional case of John the Baptist, who was not only a prophet but 'more than a prophet' (Lk. 7:26): last of the prophets and first of the witnesses. Just as the first chapters of St Luke stressed the Baptist's character of prophet, so the first chapter of St John is charged with his function of witness.[1] He was the prophet chosen to be the Messiah's precursor, that is to point Jesus out with his very finger; seen in this way he appears as the greatest of all witnesses.

Witness is rooted in prophecy, and therefore the latter, though necessarily transformed by the coming of the Christ and the fullness of time, did not disappear but in a new form remained at the centre of the life of God's Israel, the disciples of Jesus. Our Lord's possession of the Spirit, his prayer, and his gift of prophecy were all passed on in full measure to the Christian community.

[1] Jn. 1:7, 8, 15, 19, 32, 34.

JERUSALEM, JERUSALEM, STILL
MURDERING THE PROPHETS

THE general lines of a picture of Jesus as seen in the third gospel should now be clear: prophet-messiah, new Moses and new Elias, at one and the same time resembling and far transcending the prophets of the past; not only man of God but God's true Son in constant, prayerful conversation with his Father; the full possessor of the Holy Spirit. All this, however, is only part of the third gospel's central theme, it is only a still picture representing no more than the Galilean ministry. But Luke's plot centres on Jerusalem not Galilee, and far from giving a still picture it presents us with a powerful and tragic drama. As prophet, Jesus must receive the treatment of a prophet: be persecuted by the Achabs and Jezabels of his time. As Messiah, he must journey to Jerusalem and the temple as Zacharias and Malachy had prophesied. Jerusalem turns Jezabel and the central theme of the third gospel is the clash of Jesus and Jerusalem.

The prelude is Jesus' visit to Nazareth, placed by Luke at the very beginning of the public ministry. This incident has exceptional importance in pre-figuring the whole gospel plot.

He came to Nazareth, where he had been brought up; and he

went into the synagogue there, as his custom was, on the sabbath day, and stood up to read. The book given to him was the book of the prophet Isaias; so he opened it, and found the place where the words ran: The Spirit of the Lord is upon me; he has anointed me, and sent me out to preach the gospel to the poor, to restore the broken-hearted; to bid the prisoners go free, and the blind have sight; to set the oppressed at liberty, to proclaim a year when men may find acceptance with the Lord. Then he shut the book, and gave it back to the attendant, and sat down. All those who were in the synagogue fixed their eyes on him, and thus he began speaking to them, This scripture which I have read in your hearing is to-day fulfilled. All bore testimony to him and were astonished at the gracious words which came from his mouth; Why, they said, is not this the son of Joseph? Then he said to them, No doubt you will tell me, as the proverb says, Physician, heal thyself; do here in thy own country all that we have heard of thy doing at Capharnaum. And he said, Believe me, no prophet finds acceptance in his own country. Why, you may be sure of this, there were many widows among the people of Israel in the days of Elias, when a great famine came over all the land, after the heavens had remained shut for three years and six months, but Elias was not sent to any of these. He was sent to a widow woman in Sarepta, which belongs to Sidon. And there were many lepers among the people of Israel in the days of the prophet Eliseus; but it was none of them, it was Naaman the Syrian, who was made clean. All those who were in the synagogue were full of indignation at hearing this; they rose up and thrust him out of the city, and took him up to the brow of the hill on which their city was built, to throw him over it. But he passed through the midst of them, and so went on his way (4:16–30).

Historically here, as elsewhere, Luke's plan is artificial; he is grouping together two or even three visits to Nazareth as if they were one, for obviously the astonishment at Jesus' gracious words was not on the same occasion as the attempt to murder him; further, this scene is placed first in the ministry but the sentence 'all that we have heard of thy doing at Capharnaum' shows that historically it was not so. But this account of the visit to Nazareth does not aim at the mere narration of historical fact; it is meant to do much more, to sum up in advance the whole theme of the gospel: Nazareth is Israel. Jesus, forcefully depicted as the prophet in the tradition of Elias and Eliseus, comes to preach the gospel of salvation in Nazareth, which symbolizes Israel precisely as being Jesus' *own* city, his own people; what is done at Nazareth will be done in all Israel at Jerusalem. It is his own that reject him; they thrust him out of the city, they will not be evangelized by him. And he, rejected by his own, turns to the Gentiles (symbolized by Capharnaum) even as Elias and Eliseus did. The immediate sense of Jesus' reference to the miracles of Elias and Eliseus was the unexpectedness of God's gifts, a frequent Old and New Testament theme. The people of Nazareth doubtless looked to benefit from the unusual fortune of having a prophet among their young men: very human plans, but—Jesus tells them— not divine ones. God remains sovereignly free, and Jesus performs his miracles unexpectedly at Capharnaum just as Elias and Eliseus performed theirs outside Israel. This is a perfectly natural and historically authentic saying of Jesus.[1] Luke rightly saw a fuller sense in the saying. The principle to which Jesus appealed had a far wider application, and the reference to Naaman and the widow of Sarepta quite naturally pointed to the calling of the Gentiles, just as the behaviour of Nazareth pointed to the behaviour of all Jewry.[2]

[1] Whatever Creed may say, *The Gospel according to St Luke*, pp. 65–6.
[2] Hence on the one hand we need not agree with those such as Creed, who

The visit to Nazareth is followed by the record of the Galilean ministry, carried out around Capharnaum. For the most part Luke follows Mark in this section, and I do not need to examine it in detail. It is the record of Jesus' prophetical works, which begin with the exorcism of an unclean spirit, and they serve as visible signs of his power and authority; chief among them is that great miracle, of which Luke alone tells us, the raising to life of the son of the widow of Naim. It is the record of his preaching of the kingdom of God, of repentance, the forgiveness of sins and sincerity of life. The period culminates in the revelation of Jesus' future sufferings and glory. 'The Son of man, he said, is to be much ill-used, and rejected by the elders and chief priests and scribes, and be put to death, and rise again on the third day' (9:22); this is the first of the prophecies of the Passion and is immediately followed by another of Jesus' future glory: 'If anyone is ashamed of acknowledging me and my words, the Son of man will be ashamed to acknowledge him, when he comes in his glory, with his Father and the holy angels to glorify him' (9:26). These words about suffering and glory are confirmed soon after by the mysterious experience of the Transfiguration, at once the climax of the Galilean ministry and a revelation of what is about to happen in Judaea; with the Transfiguration passed, we enter on the 'journey narrative' of the third gospel.

This, the central section of Luke's gospel, gives us a series of incidents not otherwise mentioned in the gospels, placed within the framework of a journey up to Jerusalem; this single

---

reject the historicity of this incident as described by Luke, nor on the other need we follow Stonehouse (*The Witness of Luke to Christ*) in denying an allusion here to the gentile mission. History and symbolism in the New Testament are not mutually exclusive, but mutually explanatory.

journey to the holy city is central to the whole of Luke's plot, and its significance has now to be examined. First of all, it is important to notice that Luke's gospel speaks of only one journey to Jerusalem, there is no suggestion whatsoever of more than one; hence a division of this central section into the first, second and third journeys to Jerusalem, as given for instance in the Desclée Latin Bible and the English Westminster version, is quite gratuitous and foreign to the thought of St Luke.[1]

The journey to Jerusalem begins in 9:51: 'He set his face steadfastly towards the way that led to Jerusalem.' From this moment the whole of Jesus' life and ministry is Jerusalem-bound; and he goes there, in fulfilment of prophecy, as himself messiah and prophet. The phrase calls to mind the last journey of Elias, but also Isaias' words on the prophet servant of the Lord: 'The Lord God is my helper: therefore am I not confounded. Therefore have I set my face as a most hard rock' (Is. 50:7). The idea of the Jerusalem journey is emphatically repeated in the two following verses: 'And he sent messengers before him, who came into a Samaritan village, to make all in readiness. But the Samaritans refused to receive him, because his journey was in the direction of Jerusalem' (9:52–3).[2] All the narrative of the subsequent chapters has for background

[1] The arguments to the contrary advanced by Canon Louis Girard, in *L'évangile des voyages de Jésus* (Paris, 1951), are not, to my mind, convincing.

[2] But they did not refuse to receive his disciples when their journey lay away from Jerusalem. For Samaria's reception of the word see Acts 8. The apostles needed to go forth from Jerusalem to witness in Samaria (Acts 1:8); it is noticeable that there were no Samaritans in Jerusalem at Pentecost. However, once past the great divide of Jesus' death, going up to Jerusalem ceased to be such a bugbear for the Samaritans and Luke can say of the apostles as he could not say of their master, 'they began their journey back to Jerusalem, carrying the gospel into many Samaritan villages' (Acts 8:25).

the recurrent strain of the progress to Jerusalem. Jesus is making his way towards Jerusalem, going up to Jerusalem, almost arrived at Jerusalem in 13:22, 17:11, 18:31, 19:11, 19:28. Yet it is clear from the geographical and time details given that this is not one single historical journey, any more than the visit to Nazareth was one single historical visit.[1] Luke has assembled a good deal of information from various sources on Our Lord's life and has ordered them within the artificial framework of a journey to Jerusalem.[2] But artificial does not mean mistaken. Nor is it unimportant. Luke is indeed following Matthew and Mark in speaking of only one visit of Jesus to Jerusalem and making Jesus' ministry consist of one Galilean period followed by one Judaean period; but neither Matthew nor Mark have anything of Luke's concern about the journey up to Jerusalem, which has for Luke ceased to be a primarily geographical matter. Once we grasp the fact of Luke's preoccupation with Jesus' going up to Jerusalem we have to ask the reason for it, the significance of it, and hence too the significance of Jerusalem.

The first striking thing about Jerusalem in the New Testament is its name: rather, its two names, Hierosolyma and Jerusalem. What, if any, was the point of using one rather than the other? Hierosolyma (the Greek form) is always used by

1 See Vaganay's treatment of this point, *Le Problème Synoptique*, pp. 106–7.

2 On this M. Goguel remarks in *Introduction au Nouveau Testament*, I (Paris, 1923), p. 481 : 'The detailed analysis that we have made of the fragment proper to Luke shows us then that there is no question of a homogeneous bloc, but of a compilation of disparate elements. Luke has tried to link them up in a journey narrative leading Jesus from Galilee to Jerusalem; but he has been able to realise his plan only very imperfectly. What confirms the artificial and fictitious character of what one calls nowadays the journey narrative is that at its close . . . we find ourselves back at the point where Luke had abandoned the thread of Mark's story.'

Matthew (with one exception), Mark and John; it is also found four times in the third gospel, frequently in Acts, and three times in the Epistle to the Galatians. Jerusalem (the Hebrew form) occurs once in Matthew, frequently in the third gospel and Acts, and also in Romans, 1 Corinthians, Galatians, Hebrews and the Apocalypse. St Luke is the only New Testament writer who frequently makes use of both forms. St. Paul's use of the two in Galatians is precise and important: Hierosolyma is a geographical name, Jerusalem a theological one.[1] Moreover Hebrews and the Apocalypse,[2] treating like Galatians of the heavenly Jerusalem, and hence speaking theologically and not geographically, also use 'Jerusalem'. The gospels, on the other hand, are clearly concerned above all with the geographical place, and hence it may be explained that Matthew, Mark and John use the form Hierosolyma. This distinction between the two words, on the basis of the theological or the geographical preoccupation of the writer, may not, however, even outside St Luke's books, entirely explain the use of the two forms. St Paul in Romans and 1 Corinthians uses the Jerusalem form five times, four of them seemingly in a primarily geographical context; the fifth is different: Paul tells

[1] There are five texts in Galatians:

1:17. I did not go up to Hierosolyma to see those who had been apostles longer than myself.

1:18. Then, when three years had passed, I did go up to Hierosolyma, to visit Peter.

2:1. Then, after an interval of fourteen years, once again I went up to Hierosolyma with Barnabas.

4:25. Mount Sinai, in Arabia, has the same meaning in the allegory as Jerusalem, the Jerusalem which exists here and now; an enslaved city, whose children are slaves.

4:26. Whereas our mother is the heavenly Jerusalem, a city of freedom.

[2] Heb. 12:22. Apoc. 3:12; 21:2; 21:10.

the Romans that 'My own work has been to complete the preaching of Christ's gospel, in a wide sweep from Jerusalem as far as Illyricum' (Rom. 15 : 19). This also may seem a purely geographical statement but it is not really, for Paul's preaching did not actually begin in Jerusalem; he writes 'from Jerusalem' and not 'from Damascus' or 'from Antioch' because it was of the theological nature of the evangelical preaching ordered by Jesus to begin at Jerusalem (Lk. 24:47; Acts 1:8) and Paul's mission was based on these instructions of the Lord. The other four references[1] all concern the collection Paul was making for the Church of Jerusalem, and even here theology was much to the fore : the collection was being made by the Gentile churches for that of Jerusalem on account of the latter's especial ecclesiological position and as a proof of goodwill between people who did not always see eye to eye on theological questions. So we may conclude that—outside St Luke—the one has a fairly definite theological, the other a geographical connotation; it is noteworthy that St Matthew's sole use of Jerusalem ('Jerusalem, Jerusalem, still murdering the prophets' 23:37) is very clearly theological. We would expect St Luke to abide by this general, and in particular Pauline, usage.

The name Jerusalem occurs 68 times in Luke (Gospel 27, Acts 41), the name Hierosolyma 28 times (Gospel 4, Acts 24). St Luke then manifestly shows a preference for Jerusalem over Hierosolyma, in this following St Paul.[2] Without doubt Jerusalem is by far the more important form : every use of Hierosolyma is for a clearly geographical indication, not one occurring in a text of the first importance. All the especially significant texts use the form Jerusalem. Twice Luke has taken a text

[1] Rom. 15 :25, 26, 31; 1 Cor. 16:3.
[2] St Paul's ratio (including Hebrews) is: Jerusalem 8, Hierosolyma 3.

from Mark or Matthew in which the name occurs, but has changed the form from Hierosolyma to Jerusalem. One is an insignificant geographical reference (6:17), the other a text of great importance (18:31). In general it is hardly disputable that his use of the Jerusalem form, particularly in the gospel, gives the city a special theological significance in his story.[1]

To turn from the word to the reality, one may say that Jerusalem has a double character in St Luke's thought. It is the sacred city of God, the city of David and the temple, the place destined by prophecy for the Messiah's visit and reception. But it is also the city which constantly rejects the prophets, and finally the prophet-messiah, Jesus; on account of this, its original character will be lost.

When Jesus makes his way towards Jerusalem, he is fully aware that he is travelling to the faithless city that is to reject him, yet he goes there because it remains the city of God until it finally does so. It is the object of his tenderest love (13:34; 19:42), and the deepest tragedy of the third gospel is not that of the crucified Messiah, it is the tragedy of the city which has failed to recognize its Lord. Luke was well aware of Jerusalem's holiness, and this is strikingly clear in his two first chapters; what he wished to stress was the other side—not what it had been, but what it became; and there was for him an intimate connection between Jesus' death and the very idea of Jerusalem. The two are linked, even before the journey narrative begins, in the account of the Transfiguration when Jesus spoke with Moses and Elias 'of the death [exodus] which he was to achieve

---

[1] St Luke's criterion of use is not always clear; at times he seems to use one form or the other quite indiscriminately, as in Acts 8. It would be wrong to force the texts into a rigid pattern which they do not possess, and one cannot press their significance in every individual case.

at Jerusalem' (9:31). Luke alone mentions this subject of their conversation. The strange word used—Exodus—instead of referring directly to Jesus' death, seems to suggest the whole sweep of his departure from this world, death included.[1] At the moment of the Transfiguration Jesus, the prophet successor of Moses and Elias, is already joined with his death in Jerusalem.

From now on Jesus advances towards death in Jerusalem with resolution. Verse 9:51 does more than mark the beginning of the journey narrative, for the phrase 'set his face steadfastly' not only reminds us of the servant of the Lord of Isaias, it also indicates the firm determination which gives meaning to the whole prolonged journey to Jerusalem, indeed to the entire public ministry culminating in this 'visitation' of the city. The reason for the journey, the point of Jesus' firm resolution, is to be found in its end and achievement: 'the time was drawing near for his assumption.'[2] The coming drama weighs on the whole narrative and it is not surprising to find that other references to the journey Jerusalemwards are linked up with prophecies of the Passion: 'Now we are going up to Jerusalem, and all that has been written by the prophets about the Son of Man is to be accomplished. He will be given up to the Gentiles, and mocked, and beaten, and spat upon; they will scourge him, and then they will kill him; but on the third day he will rise again' (18:31–3).[3]

---

[1] The same word 'exodus' is used by St Irenaeus of the martyrdom of Saints Peter and Paul (*Cont. Haer.*, III, I, 1).

[2] ἀνάλημψις, a mysterious word reminding one of 'exodus': a taking away from the earth, at once death and, like that of Elias, ascension.

[3] As Vaganay remarks (op. cit., p. 253), in the central section 'the perspective of the passion is dominant, as if the journey to Jerusalem were a procession to death'. Canon Osty (*L'Evangile selon Saint Luc*, p. 19. *Bible de Jérusalem*) says that Luke 'has represented all the events of the Lord's

Jerusalem is the place where Jesus is to be martyred and depart this world; but, much more, it is that which is to martyr Jesus, 'this generation', an active force rejecting the Messiah who comes to it, and represented in particular by the pharisees and chief priests. This is made most clear by Jesus himself in two striking passages; in the first he denounces pharisees and lawyers:

> Woe upon you, for building up the tombs of the prophets, the same prophets who were murdered by your fathers; sure witness that you approve what your fathers did, since you build tombs for the men they murdered.[1] Whereupon the wisdom of God warns you, I will send my prophets and my apostles to them, and there will be some they will kill and persecute; so they will be answerable for all the blood of prophets that has been shed since the beginning of the world, from the blood of Abel to the blood of Zacharias, who was killed between the altar and the temple; yes, I tell you, this generation will be held answerable for it (11:47–51).

Again a little later Jesus said to the pharisees in words of fearful force:

> Today and tomorrow and the next day I must go on my journeys; there is no room for a prophet to meet his death, except at Jerusalem. Jerusalem, Jerusalem, still murdering the prophets, and stoning the messengers that are sent to thee, how often have I been ready to gather thy children together, as a hen gathers her brood under her wings, and thou didst refuse it! Behold, your house is left to you, a house uninhabited (13:33–5).

---

life as driven inevitably by a mysterious force towards Jerusalem, scene of his passion and his triumph'. For the interpretation of verse 9:51 see J. Starcky, ' "Obfirmavit faciem suam ut iret Jerusalem." Sens et portée de Luc IX, 51', *Recherches de Science Religieuse*, t. xxxix (1951–2), pp. 197–202.

[1] St Stephen echoes Our Lord's words in Acts 7:51.

Here is the very heart of Luke's theology of Jerusalem; she is the spoilt one of God, to whom has been sent a long line of prophets and messengers, but she has rejected them all and become instead the adulterous city, the murderer of the prophets, the supremely fitting place for Jesus to meet his death: but only on account of this final great refusal is she herself to be rejected and left abandoned. Jesus came to the city with open arms, but Jerusalem, official Jewry, the pharisees, refused his embrace and so caused the break between the old and the new Israel, between the faithless mass of the Jewish people and the faithful remnant of the little flock.

What were the reasons behind the attitude of the pharisees towards Jesus? Of course their lack of faith was above all the moral and religious failure of self-satisfied churchmen, small-minded people, to find room for the new dimensions which Jesus and his teaching proclaimed. He called for a revolution of heart, a conversion from worldliness to sincerity, and they were not willing to be converted; furthermore it was because his teaching centred on himself and proclaimed himself to be the new authoritative teacher of the Jewish people that the scribes, pharisees and sadducees—the recognized leaders and teachers of the Jewish community—could not tolerate his presence in Israel. But there was more to it than this. A wider reason for the antagonism of their whole class towards Jesus lay in the fact that he was a prophet and not a scribe. 'Jerusalem, Jerusalem, still murdering the prophets'—just the one thing which these people could not endure was a prophet. There was simply no room for one in their religious economy, in which everything centred upon the law—the *Torah*—and its interpretation by skilled and learned men. For them the great prophets of the past had had a very minor part to play in sacred history; old prophets were for them but new scribes writ large, their job had been to recall people to the observance of the *Torah*, and since there were now an adequate number of far better educated scribes to fulfil this function there could be no point in any further prophets. The past prophetical contribution to the religion of Israel is summed up in one of the sayings of the Rabbis: 'Forty-eight prophets and eight prophetesses have prophesied after Moses for Israel: they have taken away nothing of what was written in the *Torah*, and they have added nothing, except for the law of the feast of Purim contained in the book of Esther.'[1] Furthermore, if a modern prophet was to be tolerated at all he could clearly have no other work than a faithful teaching of the law; but Jesus' work was quite other than this. He set himself above the law (6: 1–11; 13:10–17), and it was this that no scribe or pharisee could endure. Useless to justify his claims by miracles, for in their eyes no vision or miracle could have any force against the overwhelming authority of the *Torah* as they interpreted it; so the Rabbi Jeremias declared that 'The *Torah* having been given once for all on Sinai, we pay no attention to a heavenly voice.'[2] Evidently, then, Jesus' whole prophetical approach, both in his teaching and the proofs of his teaching, was ruled out from the start by the pharisees of Jerusalem, though it was popular enough in Galilee where the religion of the scribes had little influence. Jesus like John was a prophet and as such the pharisees had little use for either. Consequently he accused them of blindness, false moral teaching, hypocrisy and the murdering of the prophets, and they in their turn resolved to lie in wait for him and add his name to their list of victims (11:37–54).

1 Megilla 14a. Quoted by Giblet in *L'Attente du Messie*, p. 96.
2 Berak 52a. Quoted by Giblet, op. cit., p. 98.

Their chance—and his—was found in the dramatic meeting of prophet and Jerusalem. Jesus had at last arrived at the holy city after his long journey, and he entered it in all solemnity as messianic king (19:29–48). His triumphal, authoritative behaviour at once provoked the reaction of his enemies, and his scouring of the temple was followed by the question of authority: 'What is the authority by which thou doest these things?'; the battle was begun (20:1–7). Jesus refused to answer this impudent demand of priests and scribes; instead he told them a parable, that of the unfaithful vine-dressers. It was aimed at his interrogators and in hardly veiled terms Jesus summed up in it the whole of sacred history and its culmination in himself and their rejection of him: He is the corner-stone discarded by the builders (20:9–18). The priests and scribes would tolerate no more; afraid on account of the people of arresting Jesus there and then for sedition, they nevertheless made up their minds: 'They would hand him over to the supreme authority of the governor' (20:19–20). From this moment the issue was decided, though outwardly the fight could continue; to trap Jesus they gave him rope and asked him questions; they awaited an opportune moment to make his arrest; they welcomed the traitor. Jesus on his side denounced his enemies, again and more solemnly pronounced the doom of Jerusalem, and then—after eating his last meal with his disciples and leaving them the enduring memorial of his freely-accepted Passion—he prepared in prayer for the end. The soldiers arrived, the long hours of mockery followed, the trials before the Sanhedrin, before Pilate and Herod, and then on Calvary the death of the cross. This was the fate reserved for the king who had come in the name of the Lord.

Those are the bare bones of the story; in his account of them

Luke kept close to the historical order, and his narrative is very similar to those of Matthew and Mark. Nevertheless he has his personal variations. He replaces the drying-up of the fig-tree, which in Matthew and Mark symbolizes the sterility of Jerusalem, by an immediate prophecy of the city's destruction on account of her blindness. He passes rapidly over the scouring of the temple and he also omits a few minor passages in Matthew and Mark which might seem to digress from the dramatic unity of the narrative. But he is describing the same events in the same way and for their interpretation largely relies upon the same Old Testament passages—texts for the most part used already by Jesus himself.[1]

The immediate culmination of the great journey is to be found in Jesus' triumphal entry into Jerusalem and the Temple:

> They brought the colt to Jesus, and spread out their garments on it, and bade Jesus mount. As he went, they strewed the road with their garments; and when he drew near the descent of mount Olivet, the whole company of his disciples began rejoicing and praising God for all the miracles they had seen. Blessed is the king, they said, who comes in the name of the Lord; peace and glory in heaven above.[2] Some of the Pharisees who were among the multitude said to him, Master, rebuke thy disciples; but he answered, I tell you, if they should keep silence, the stones will cry out instead. . . . Then he went into the temple, and began driving out those who sold and bought there; it is written, he told them, My house is a house of prayer;

[1] For the Old Testament framework of the evangelical recitals in this section see J. W. Doeve's valuable study 'Purification du Temple et Dessèchement du Figuier', *New Testament Studies*, May 1955, pp. 297–308.

[2] Mgr Knox has 'Peace on earth and glory above', thus imitating Luke 2:14. What the text actually says is 'Peace in heaven and glory in the heights'.

and you have made it into a den of thieves. And he taught in the temple daily (19:35–40, 45–7).

Luke has substituted 'king' for Mark's 'kingdom', making more explicit the fulfilment of the prophecy of Zacharias 9:9; while his insertion of 'Peace and glory in heaven above' recall Luke 2:14. The whole of this passage is full of the purest Lucan spirit—peace, the rejoicing and praising of the disciples over Christ's acts of power, glory, the contrast between the company of the disciples and the company of the pharisees, prayer, the evocation of prophecy. The prophecies in question here are Malachy, Zacharias and Psalm 117. Malachy, after speaking of the mission of the precursor, foretold the Messiah's arrival at the temple of God.

> And presently the Lord whom you seek, and the angel of the testament whom you desire shall come to his temple. Behold he cometh, saith the Lord of hosts. And who shall be able to think of the day of his coming? and who shall stand to see him? For he is like a refining fire and like the fuller's herb. And he shall sit refining and cleansing, and he shall purify the sons of Levi and shall refine them as gold and as silver: and they shall offer sacrifices to the Lord in justice (Mal. 3:1–3).

To Malachy's vision of the visitation and cleansing of the temple is added Zacharias' picture of the Messiah's joyful yet humble entry into the city: 'Rejoice greatly, O daughter of Sion, shout for joy, O daughter of Jerusalem: Behold thy king will come to thee, the just and saviour. He is poor and riding upon an ass, and upon a colt, the foal of an ass' (Zach. 9:9). With this in mind Luke (like Jn. 12:13) included the royal title in the disciples' refrain taken from Psalm 117:26: 'Blessed be he that cometh in the name of the Lord'. At this joyful cry the pharisees, of course, at once began their usual carping

8

complaints: 'Master, rebuke thy disciples'. But the time for keeping the messianic secret was long past and Jesus roundly replied to them 'I tell you, if they should keep silence, the stones will cry out instead' (19:39–40). To this same psalm Jesus himself returned next day in dispute with the pharisees. He had told them of the vine-dressers, how they killed the well-beloved son of the man who had planted the vineyard.

> This is the heir, let us kill him so that his inheritance may pass into our hands. And they thrust him out of the vineyard and killed him. And now, what will the owner of the vineyard do to them? He will come and make an end of those vine-dressers, and give his vineyard to others. God forbid, they said, when they heard that (20:14–16).

The language of parable was too thin to conceal for a moment Jesus' meaning, and the words of the vine-dressers too close to the thoughts of the Jews. The vineyard, as every reader of Isaias 5 knew, was Israel; scribes and priests the vine-dressers; Jesus himself is the Son and in his audience are his murderers; dropping parable, he appeals to Psalm 117:22 which becomes from this moment one of the key texts of Christian theology.

> He fastened his eyes on them, and said, Why then, what is the meaning of those words which have been written, The very stone which the builders rejected has become the chief stone at the corner? If ever a man falls against that stone, he will break his bones; if it falls upon him, it will grind him to powder (20:17–18).

With that, the stage is set. The combatants are decided. Jesus has come up to Jerusalem with no other aim than to die and so effect his glorious 'exodus' from this world, preparatory to the descent of the Spirit on his disciples; while his enemies, priests and scribes, have now finally decided to kill him. The days of the pasch approach. Jesus' firm resolution to meet his death in Jerusalem is manifested in his desire to eat this final pasch before his Passion: 'With desire I have desired to eat this pasch with you, before I suffer' (22:15). It becomes the sacrament of his Passion to be re-enacted by his disciples, the new alliance in his blood, pledge of the kingdom's coming. With it we are in the moment of the final drama: the kingdom which the Father has given to Jesus he hands on with his body and blood to his disciples (22:29). There follows Jesus' agony in the garden, the sweat of his blood, the comforting of an angel. 'It was fitting that Christ should suffer' (24:26): this was the rejection of the corner-stone, the dereliction of the Servant of the Lord required for the salvation of God's people. Luke speaks less of the sufferings of the Passion than Matthew, Mark or John, though he does not conceal them and he knew their fruitfulness. But he shows Jesus as the well-beloved Son to the end, praying to the Father, prophesying to the women and to the repentant thief, enduringly merciful. He freely died, it was for this that he had come up to Jerusalem, on account of this that he instituted the sacrament of the Eucharist, as it was this that the prophets had foretold. He had accepted the lot of the well-beloved son, to be thrust out of the vineyard, out of the city, and killed.

If the Passion and cross were Jesus' free choice, they were also Jerusalem's responsibility and guilt. He was the son, but they were the vine-dressers. Their fate could be no less certain than his: the owner of the vineyard would come and 'make an end of those vine-dressers'. At this moment the old order is no more; the veil of the temple is rent in two, and Jesus himself has taken the place of the temple. Jerusalem is no longer the Holy City, the physical sons of Abraham no longer the Israel of God. The visible sacrament of this spiritual rejection is the city's destruction, 'Your house is left to you, a house uninhabited'. In the third gospel the prophecies of Jerusalem's destruction are developed at length,[1] and the punishment of the faithless city is shown with peculiar clarity, 'and all because thou didst not recognise the time of my visiting thee' (19:44). Now the very clarity of these prophecies on the fall of Jerusalem has been a cause of scandal for the Rationalists. For instance, Luke alone mentions Jerusalem by name in the eschatological discourses; instead of Mark's 'When you see the abomination of desolation standing where it should never stand (let him who reads this, recognise what it means), then those who are in Judaea must take refuge in the mountains' (Mk. 13:14) he has 'When you see Jerusalem surrounded by armies, be sure that the time has come when she will be laid waste. Then those who are in Judaea must take refuge in the mountains' (21:20–1). This sort of thing has made the Rationalists allot to the third gospel a date after the destruction of Jerusalem in A.D. 70, but this is really very unlikely; Harnack rightly insisted on a date about A.D. 63. Luke's particular stress on Jerusalem's siege and destruction is easily understood once we grasp the continuity of the Jerusalem theme throughout his work. His purpose required as that of the two first evangelists did not, that Jerusalem, the holy-unholy city, should be mentioned by name in the prophecies of woe.

Furthermore it is quite wrong to think that Luke's passages give an eye-witness or contemporary account of Titus' taking of the city. Here, if anywhere, his language is that of the Old Testament, and must be understood as such.[2] Above all, with-

---

[1] 19:41–4; 21:20–4; 23:28–30.

[2] See J. Doeve, op. cit.; C. H. Dodd writes, 'Not only are the two Lucan

out chapters 6 and 7 of Jeremias, it is not possible to explain St Luke's ideas about the rejection and destruction of Jerusalem and the temple, in which the Jews so falsely put their trust. 'Trust not in lying words, saying: the temple of the Lord, the temple of the Lord, it is the temple of the Lord' (Jer. 7:4). Luke's great concern was to draw Christians and Jews away from centredness on the Jerusalem temple, which had become a dead thing, and he found a great ally in Jeremias. Detail for detail these two chapters of Jeremias provided the groundwork for Jesus' prophecies on the fate of Jerusalem.

Take first Luke 13:34–5:

> Jerusalem, Jerusalem, still murdering the prophets, and stoning the messengers that are sent to thee, how often have I been ready to gather thy children together, as a hen gathers her brood under her wings, and thou didst refuse it! Behold, your house is left to you, a house uninhabited. I tell you, you shall see nothing of me until the time comes, when you will be saying, Blessed is he that comes in the name of the Lord.

The first part of this passage reminds one of Jeremias 7:25–6: 'No day dawned but I was at work betimes, sending my servants to prophesy to them, but still they would not listen, still hearing they gave me none'; the next part of Luke has an obvious parallel in Jeremias 6:8, 'Jerusalem, be warned in time; else my love thou shalt forfeit, and I will make a ruin of thee, a land uninhabited.' The last words of Our Lord in St

oracles (i.e. xix, 42–4, xxi, 20–4) composed *entirely* from the language of the Old Testament, but the conception of the coming disaster which the author has in mind is a generalized picture of the fall of Jerusalem as imaginatively presented by the prophets. So far as any historical event has coloured the picture, it is not Titus' capture of Jerusalem in A.D. 70, but Nebuchadnezzar's capture in 586 B.C.' ('The Fall of Jerusalem and the Abomination of Desolation', *Journal of Roman Studies*, 1947, p. 52).

Luke's passage refer to the coming entry into Jerusalem and therefore link the whole passage up with Luke 19:41–6, which runs as follows:

> And when he drew near, seeing the city, he wept over it saying: If thou hadst known, and that in this thy day, the things that are to thy peace: but now they are hidden from thy eyes. For the days shall come upon thee: and thy enemies shall cast a trench about thee and compass thee round and straiten thee on every side. And beat thee flat to the ground, and thy children who are in thee. And they shall not leave in thee a stone upon a stone; because thou hast not known the time of thy visitation. And entering into the temple, he began to cast out them that sold therein and them that bought. Saying to them: It is written: My house is the house of prayer. But you have made it a den of thieves!

Here Jesus' first words recall Jeremias 6:13–14: 'From the prophet even to the priests, all are guilty of deceit, saying: Peace, peace. And there was no peace.' Luke 19:43—'Thy enemies shall cast a trench about thee and compass thee round' —is a reminder of Jeremias 6:6, 'Thus saith the Lord of hosts. Hew down her trees, cast up a trench about Jerusalem.' Luke 19:44 links up with two passages of Jeremias: 'Behold I will bring destruction upon this people, by which fathers and sons together shall fall' (6:21) and 'They shall fall among them that fall: in the time of their visitation they shall fall down, saith the Lord' (6:15). Finally, in the scouring of the temple, Jeremias 7:11, referring to the temple become a den of thieves, is explicitly quoted.

Luke's whole doctrine finds its sources in the teaching of the great prophets on Jerusalem's fornication ('Peccatum peccavit Jerusalem', Lam. 1:8) and consequent punishment, developed especially in Jeremias and Ezechiel; and to appreciate it we have to enter into his forceful understanding of the fulfilment of the Old Testament in this rejection of Jerusalem and consequent calling of the Gentiles. For that was what followed the clash between builders and corner-stone: the vine-owner will 'give his vineyard to others', the suffering servant will become a light to the Gentiles.

Jerusalem is punished, the door of salvation is opened to the peoples of the whole world. If Israel and Jerusalem are represented in the gospel story especially by the pharisees, the Gentiles seem to be symbolized by the publicans. The pharisees were those 'who had confidence in themselves, thinking they had won acceptance with God, and despised the rest of the world [lit: others]' (18:9); above all they despised the publicans (15:1-2). The contempt of pharisees for publicans within the nation is paralleled by the contempt of Jews for Gentiles on the supra-national level. But as it is not the pharisee but the publican who is made pleasing to God (18:10-14) so not the Jew but the Gentile receives salvation. This is made very clear in chapter 19, in the contrast between Jericho and Jerusalem: Zacchaeus, the publican of Jericho, welcomes the Lord and Jesus can say, 'Today, salvation has been brought to this house; he too is a son of Abraham' (19:9); but the pharisees of Jerusalem refuse to welcome Jesus, and become a subject not for rejoicing but for tears (19:39-42). Jerusalem rejects her Lord and Israel is rejected; Jericho welcomes the Lord, and salvation is thrown open to the Gentiles, who become the new sons of Abraham, sons in faith. This is the final act in the drama, an act which will be more stressed when the drama is re-enacted with Paul as chief character, but which is already quite clearly envisaged in the Gospel. The Jews, profitless vine-dressers, are to be cast out of the kingdom while 'Others will come from the east and the west, the north and the south, to take their ease in the kingdom of God' (13:29). For the Jews, with all their sense of an exclusive revelation, this was to be the hardest punishment of all.

The deep theological sense of the journey narrative in the third gospel is now clear. It brings together the two participants in the drama of the Passion, history's most decisive event: Jesus and Jerusalem. St Luke brings out the respective parts which the two played in this event, the freedom and deliberateness of Jesus in his advance towards the cross, the guilt of Jerusalem faithful only to her faithlessness. So as to stress this, to bring to the light the central point of Jesus' life, all other visits to Jerusalem during the public ministry are ignored. For Luke there is only one, one journey, one visitation, one supreme and decisive encounter culminating in Jesus' martyrdom and Jerusalem's destruction; and it is always for Jerusalem, not for Jesus, that one must weep. Jesus cried over the misguided city immediately on catching sight of her (19:41); and at the supreme hour of the Passion, when official Jerusalem seems triumphant and Jesus on his way to a criminal's death, he feels precisely as at the moment of his greatest earthly triumph: 'It is not for me that you should weep, daughters of Jerusalem; you should weep for yourselves and for your children' (23:28).[1] Jesus, with the eye of a prophet, saw what was hidden from both adversary and sympathizer: that the stone rejected by the builders had fallen upon them and was about to grind them to powder.

Yet the early chapters of the third gospel give us a very different picture of Jerusalem. Whereas in the public ministry

[1] The women's weeping of Luke 23:27 reminds one of Zacharias 12:11.

the whole atmosphere is of strife, of division between the city and her Lord, the atmosphere of the first chapters is one of idyllic peace and unity. Harsh episodes such as the massacre of the Innocents and the flight into Egypt are ignored. Instead we find Jerusalem and the temple faithfully accepting its new-born Lord. Zachary, Elizabeth, above all Mary, are examples of the true Israel. In the temple Simeon takes Jesus in his arms, Anna gives thanks, the learned doctors listen with amazement to the answers of Jesus. The contrast between all this and the later chapters is very powerful, and is quite intentional; in these first chapters Luke provides the matter for a clear comparison. This is the way Jerusalem should have received its Lord, the way indicated by the sacred scriptures, the way taken by the true Israel, not official Jewry but the 'little flock' which abandoned the old Jerusalem for the new, the earthly for the heavenly. These chapters have also the important function of further stressing Jesus' fidelity to the temple.

However, at the end of these two chapters Luke records an incident—the finding in the temple—which is perhaps symbolical of what was to come.[1] Jesus goes up with his own to Jerusalem for the paschal feast as he was to go up later for the pasch of the Passion. He is separated from his people, enters into the world of his Father, and only returns to his people on the third day (compare the 'after three days' of 2:45 with 'the third day' of 24:7, 21). Now as afterwards his friends seek to find him (2:45; 24:2, 23) and fail in their understanding of what was happening (2:50; 24:25; 18:34). Now as afterwards a temporary separation of Jesus from his mother and family (the disciples receive this title by right of 8:21) is ended by

1 The parallel here suggested I owe to Dr Lampe, 'The Holy Spirit in the writings of St Luke', *Studies in the Gospels*, p. 182.

joyful reunion. This incident, together with Simeon's prophecy of the 'sign which men will refuse to acknowledge' and the sword which shall pierce Mary's soul, are the first hints of that tragic drama in which, across Jesus' rejection and death in Jerusalem, the Old Israel goes down and the New is born— 'This child is destined to bring about the fall of many and the rise of many in Israel' (2:34).

St Luke tells us of one other and very mysterious visit of Jesus to Jerusalem, that in 4:9–13, when Satan led him there and placed him on a pinnacle of the temple; it is for Luke the third and greatest of the messianic temptations for which Jesus had been led by the Spirit into the desert. In his narrative he has changed the Matthaean order of the temptations, placing this one—instead of the high mountain—at the end for climax. Matthew placed the temptation on the mountain last because it was for him the most significant: 'Once more, the devil took him up to the top of an exceedingly high mountain, from which he shewed him all the kingdoms of the world and the glory of them, and said, I will give thee all these if thou wilt fall down and worship me' (Mt. 4:8–9). Matthew's gospel is that of the kingdom. Here on the mountain Jesus rejects a false kingdom and immediately afterwards (5:1) goes up another mountain to teach of the coming of the true one. The same gospel ends on a mountain in Galilee with Jesus' proclamation of his kingdom to his apostles and the gift he has received of all authority in heaven and on earth. But this viewpoint is foreign to the mind of Luke, whose equivalent to the sermon on the Mountain of Matthew is a sermon on the plain (Lk. 6:17) not, as Matthew's is, explicitly concerned with the kingdom: while the third gospel ends not on a mountain in Galilee but just outside Jerusalem. The temptation order of the two gospels (like their

Resurrection narratives) is to be explained by the chief pre-occupations of their writers—Jerusalem in the one case, the Kingdom in the other. In this temptation visit to the temple of Jerusalem Jesus refuses the role of false messiah; and when he visits her again it will be as true Messiah, not making his presence known by a pointless miracle but arriving, in accordance with prophecy, humbly upon an ass.

We can see now that the principal act of the third gospel is reached only after a series of preludes. First of all, the old and faithful Israel is described, in contrast with the scribes and pharisees who later came, and so disastrously, to represent Jerusalem. Secondly, in the mysterious incident of the boy Jesus' visit to the temple, a type of his later Jerusalem journey is suggested. Thirdly, following Jesus' messianic baptism, the temptation visit shows us the kind of messiah which Jesus was not. Fourthly, in the scene at Nazareth with which the public ministry begins, the whole course of Jesus' ministry and Israel's reaction to him is clearly symbolized.

What may seem strange is that after all the *sturm und drang* of the central part of the gospel, we arrive back at the end in an atmosphere strangely similar to the beginning. In chapter 24 all is again at peace, the Passion seems but a passing phase, and after the Ascension the apostles 'went back full of joy to Jerusalem, where they spent their time continually in the temple, praising and blessing God' (24:52–3; see also Acts 2:46–7). This re-emergence of the temple reminds one of the similar phenomenon in the final chapters of Ezechiel (40–8). Yet in so far as the visible temple is in question, this was not destined to last. The apostles must wait in the city, but only until clothed with power from on high, then they must go forth to all nations. In fact the Jerusalem in which they now abide, praising and blessing God, is already the new Jerusalem, 'our mother, a city of freedom', as is that of the last chapters of Ezechiel when re-interpreted in the Apocalypse. The temple veil was rent for ever in two at the moment of Our Lord's death, and this could mean no less than that the visible temple of Jerusalem was God's house no more.[1]

[1] See Appendix: 'The Holy City'.

8

LEAVE JERUSALEM AND GO AFAR
UNTO THE GENTILES

WHAT was sown in Jesus was reaped in the Church. We find
in the Acts of the Apostles, especially in St Paul's life, both the
continuation and the consequence of Jesus' life and death. The
record of events given there would be a very meagre one if
the book had been intended as a history of the apostolic Church.
But it was not: its title is misleading. We have no right to
presume from it that the apostles, other than Peter and Paul,
did not carry on an active and fruitful apostolate both in and
out of Judaea. Peter and Paul, it is true, might seem to receive
equal honours, half the book each.[1] They both witness; both
are persecuted by high priests and kings; both are delivered

[1] I have said little about the sources Luke used for writing the Acts. He
himself witnessed most of what is described in the second part of the book,
but for the first 12 chapters he was dependent on the testimony of others,
written or oral. There is little agreement as to just what sources Luke used,
how they were divided and how much was written, but it seems worth while
to give briefly the conclusions Mgr Cerfaux reached in a careful study of the
question ('La Première Partie du Livre des Actes', *Ephemerides Theologicae
Lovanienses* (1936), pp. 667–91).

He distinguished three chief groups of sources:

1. A fairly well-defined document deriving from the Church of Jerusalem
and covering Acts 2:41—5:40.

miraculously from prison; both set out from Jerusalem, and both convert the Gentiles; both raise the dead. Peter is given a deftly suggested primacy, but Paul is Luke's hero and the centre of his interest.

Yet it would be almost as wrong to think of the book as a chronicle of the acts of Peter and Paul, with a preference for the latter, as to call it a history of the apostolic Church. The real aim is far deeper: it is to bring out the meaning in the Church's early development and the inner theological movement of the apostolate from Jerusalem to the Gentiles. This is why the book centres on the apostle of the Gentiles *par excellence*, St Paul. The marked concentration of attention on the latter has both a personal and a theological explanation; in fact the two come together, for the nature of Paul's conversion identified him personally with the apostolate to the Gentiles and its theological justification. This conversion, it must be noted, is about the most significant event in the whole book, its importance being brought out by means of a triple description.[1]

---

2. A group of traditions (partly written, partly oral) belonging probably to the Church of Caesarea, a community of universally-minded Judaeo-Christians. These cover: (i) 2:1–47. Pentecost. (ii) 8:1–40 (excluding 14–25). Acts of Philip. (iii) 9:1–30. Saul's conversion. (iv) 9:31—11:18. Acts of Peter. (v) 12:19–23. The end of Herod.

3. Some more hellenistically-minded Antiocene documents, also in general more precise than the second group. They include the Acts of Stephen (chapters 6 and 7) and the founding of the Church of Antioch, 11:19–30.

It is with regard to the large and amorphous second group that it is most difficult to arrive at any very sure conclusion; in it too St Luke's own hand can most easily be seen, but everywhere he will have adapted his sources according to his own interests and ideas. The first 14 verses of chapter 1 is perhaps the most purely Lucan thing in these chapters.

[1] Acts 9:1–22; 22:1–21; 26:9–18.

It was an experience with two sides, but one reality. On one side it was conversion from persecuting to preaching the name of Jesus, with the consciousness of a personal relationship with Jesus which from then on directed his every thought; on the other it was a mission to the Gentiles. In Paul's person these two are one. He was not first a Christian and then a missionary later on, he was called to be both from the very first.[1]

> I heard a voice which said to me, in Hebrew, Saul, Saul, why dost thou persecute me? This is a thankless task of thine, kicking against the goad. Who art thou, Lord? I asked. And the Lord said, I am Jesus, whom Saul persecutes. Rise up, and stand on thy feet; I have shown myself to thee, that I may single thee out to serve me, as the witness of this vision thou hast had, and other visions thou wilt have of me. I will be thy deliverer from the hands of thy people, and of the Gentiles, to whom I am now sending thee. Thou shalt open their eyes, and turn them from darkness to light, from the power of Satan to God, so that they may receive, through faith in me, remission of their sins and an inheritance among the saints (26:14–18).

1 Mgr Cerfaux has pointed out that 'It is necessary to grasp the primordial importance of the apostolic idea in St Paul's consciousness. The certainty that he had a mission to accomplish made another man of him. On the road to Damascus he understood that he was the chosen one of God to carry the gospel of his Son to the Gentiles; what he calls his conversion is in reality only his vocation to the apostolate of the Gentiles within the framework of Jewish messianism. It is thus the most explicit passage of the epistles represents the event of the Damascus road: Paul likens himself to a prophet of the Old Testament, perhaps more precisely to the servant of God of Isaias, who is besides represented with a prophet's traits; he has been set apart by God from his mother's womb for his mission, he has been "called", God has "revealed" to him his Son, having already in mind the evangelization of the Gentiles (Gal. 1:15–16)' ('Antinomie Paulinienne de la Vie Apostolique', *Mélanges Jules Lebreton*, I, p. 221).

At the very moment of his conversion he was entrusted with the greatest of missionary tasks.

The expanding character of the Church's apostolate as also its inner nature are placed before us from the very beginning of Acts: 'The Holy Spirit will come upon you, and you will receive power from him; you are to be my witnesses in Jerusalem and throughout Judaea, in Samaria, yes, and to the ends of the earth' (1:8). The apostolate begins in Jerusalem but is to be universal; it starts with the Jews but is to end with the Gentiles. It is a work of witnessing to Christ, for which the power of the Holy Spirit is required. Acts is a chronicle of the Spirit's activity, and it is this which gives unity to the two parts and renders the midway substitution of Paul for Peter a matter of secondary importance. The Spirit must work through men, and Acts is therefore also a chronicle of Christian witnessing; if Paul comes to dominate its pages, this is only possible because he has, like Peter, the character of Witness in its fullness, and is very specially and markedly guided by the Holy Spirit. The programme of 1:8—to witness in Jerusalem, Judaea and Samaria, and to the ends of the earth—is carried out personally by Paul: 'First to those in Damascus, then in Jerusalem, then to all the country of Judaea, then to the heathen, I preached repentance' (26:20), and the book ends with his witness in Rome (28:23).

The earlier incidents recorded in the book are an introduction and basis for St Paul's work: the Pentecostal gift of tongues, the speech and martyrdom of St Stephen, the baptisms of the Ethiopian eunuch and the centurion Cornelius, Peter's speech in the assembly at Jerusalem, all these lead up to the great mission pre-eminently confided to Paul—the mission that took him 'afar unto the Gentiles'. From this point of view the incident of Cornelius' conversion (chapter 10) has a quite special importance. Peter's speech to Cornelius (vv. 34–43) is in many ways a key passage for the understanding of early Christian thought, and it begins with Peter's discovery that the Gentiles too are acceptable to God. After his account of the Council of Jerusalem (chap. 15), Luke almost wholly ignores the apostolate in Jerusalem and Palestine, and if he continues to refer frequently to the conversion of Jews, yet it is always as a splinter group that he portrays those converted. What stands out of his book as clear as day is at once the steady Jewish rejection of the Church, the Gospel and Paul, and the conversion of a multitude among the Gentiles. This is made very plain, for instance, at Corinth, when Paul says to the Jews there, 'Your blood be upon your heads; I am clear of it; I will go to the Gentiles henceforward' (18:6). Or again there is the account of Paul's speech at Pisidian Antioch: 'We were bound to preach God's word to you first; but now, since you reject it, since you declare yourselves unfit for eternal life, be it so; we will turn our thoughts to the Gentiles' (13:46). But the clearest example of all is to be found in the words of Paul to the Jews at Rome which come at the very end of the book (28:25–8) and are indeed the key to what St Luke was trying to put across all along; they point the moral of the whole story:

It was a true utterance the Holy Spirit made to our fathers through the prophet Isaias:

Go to this people and tell them:

You will listen and listen, but for you there is no under- standing;

You will watch and watch, but for you there is no per- ceiving.

The heart of this people has become dull,

9

> Their ears are slow to listen,
> They keep their eyes shut,
> So that they may never see with those eyes,
> Or hear with those ears,
> Or understand with that heart,
> And turn back to me, and win healing from me.
>
> Take notice then, that this message of salvation has been sent by God to the Gentiles, and they, at least, will listen to it.

This passage gives us the theological key to the whole plot and thesis of Acts,[1] and St Paul dominates the book because its thesis can be shown forth most conveniently in and through an account of his work. This thesis is that Christianity is the fulfilment of Judaism, yet has itself a universal character, as much at home in Corinth or Rome as in Judaea; that official Jewry has rejected Christianity, and that this very rejection is the occasion, and a further reason, for the evangelization of the Gentiles. Now this is closely akin to the theme of the third gospel, as we know: Jesus did not reject Judaism, on the contrary his ministry was largely a journey up to Jerusalem,

---

1 As Harnack already remarked (*Luke the Physician*, p. 130, n. 1). A. H. N. Green-Armytage makes some worth-while remarks on the plot of Acts in his *Portrait of St Luke*, pp. 73–5: 'This is St Luke's main theme, the plot and mythos of his story, and he holds to it rigidly and ruthlessly—that Judaism is fulfilled in Christianity and the law of Moses has been superseded. There is a new Jerusalem, the Church of Christ, of which all men without exception may be citizens. It is the central doctrine of St Paul expressed in historical terms. ... Luke's treatment of the Jews is open to criticism. They constantly reject their own salvation. They murder Stephen, stone Paul, stir up unwilling Roman magistrates against the Apostles. It is a Jewish king, with Jewish approval, who kills James and imprisons Peter . . . . St Luke's story is certainly coloured by an anti-Jewish prejudice.' Mr Green-Armytage certainly touches on an important aspect of the plot of Acts, and indeed of the Gospel in these lines. But I think it should be made clear that St Luke's 'anti-Jewish prejudice' was of a very theological nature.

but it was Jerusalem that rejected him and his preaching as it had rejected other prophets before him; by so doing, it and it alone was responsible for the division between Christianity and official Jewry, while at the same time providentially opening the door through its very obduracy for the apostolate of the Gentiles. The final message of the Gospel is that repentance and the remission of sins should be preached in Christ's name to all nations (Lk. 24:47), as the final message of the Acts is that salvation has been sent by God to the Gentiles, and they, at least, will listen to it (Acts 28:28).

Without going back over the plot of the third gospel, it is here worth considering two parables which help to make clear the supreme theme running through St Luke's work. We take first Luke 20:9 18, the parable of the vine-dressers and Jesus' reference to himself as the corner-stone. It is a passage which very clearly expresses what Luke was at such pains to bring home to his readers: that the mission to the Gentiles was the inevitable sequence to the Jewish rejection of Christ; God has given his vineyard to others. As Luke says, the chief priests saw the point of the whole story, and would gladly have laid hands on Jesus there and then. However as the whole of this passage is common to Matthew and Mark, from whom St Luke borrowed it, it is not very good evidence of St Luke's personal preoccupations. It is evidence, however, of something else of the greatest importance; it is this: St Luke's theology is only an unusual stress on something which was common and primitive doctrine. His theology is seen here as the natural development of Jesus' own application to himself of the rejected corner-stone of Psalm 117.

In our second parable, however, we find Luke more on his own. It is that of the great supper (14:16–24) which can be compared with the parable of the wedding feast in Matthew (22:1–14). These two passages are normally considered together by the textual critics in spite of their wide differences,[1] but from our point of view their comparison is illuminating, for the point of the two is markedly different. The point of Matthew's parable centres on its second half, on what happened when the makeshift guests were collected from the street corners:

> When the king came in to look at the company, he saw a man there who had no wedding-garment on; My friend, he said, how didst thou come to be here without a wedding-garment? And he made no reply. Whereupon the king said to his servants, Bind him hand and foot, and cast him out into the darkness, where there shall be weeping, and gnashing of teeth. Many are called, but few are chosen (Mt. 22:11–14).

The first part of the parable, concerning the guests who refused to come and maltreated the king's servants, refers doubtless to Israel; but the stress of the parable lies more in the second part referring to the newly invited, and its moral—the kernel of Jesus' teaching here—is given in the final verse, 'Many are called but few are chosen', which refers to the second part of the story, to the man without a wedding-garment,[2] and has nothing special to do with the Jewish people as such.[3] Luke's parable has a different ending; nothing about a wedding-

---

[1] E.g. Vaganay, *Le Problème Synoptique*, p. 146.

[2] Cf. E. Boissard, O.S.B., 'Multi sunt vocati, pauci vero electi', *Revue Thomiste*, 1952, III, pp. 569–85.

[3] It is true that it is significantly placed by Matthew immediately following the parable of the vine-dressers and evidently relates to Jesus' last great clash with the Pharisees (see verse 15); but A. Jones is surely right in remarking (*A Catholic Commentary*, p. 890) that 'This parable-allegory. . . is not directed

garment, or about a selection among the newly-invited guests. When the servant came back and told his master of the guests' refusal,

> The host fell into a rage, and said to his servant, Quick, go out into the streets and lanes of the city; bring in the poor, the cripples, the blind and the lame. And when the servant told him, Sir, all has been done according to thy command, but there is room left still, the master said to the servant, Go out into the highways and hedgerows, and give them no choice but to come in, that so my house may be filled. I tell you, none of those who were first invited shall taste of my supper (Lk. 14:21-4).

Again, the moral of the story is given in the last line, but the point here is precisely the rejection of the first invited, that is to say the Jews, after their refusal of God's invitation to the supper of the kingdom; furthermore the call of the Gentiles is placed in the very strongest relief—'Give them no choice but to come in.' The point of this parable is similar to that of the vine-dressers, and it is repeated outside the parable and in the strongest terms in Luke 13:28-9: 'Weeping shall be there, and gnashing of teeth, when you see Abraham and Isaac and Jacob and all the prophets within God's kingdom, while you yourselves are cast out. Others will come from the east and the west, the north and the south, to take their ease in the kingdom of God.' This again is paralleled in Matthew (8:11-12); but it is noteworthy that the passage in Matthew follows naturally upon the story of the Centurion's faith—it is an obvious reaction to the latter; hence it has perhaps less import than in Luke, where it has a different context and a more significant one, immediately

against the Jewish leaders as such, . . . it is addressed to all and relates to the personnel of the kingdom'. In fact here, as elsewhere, Matthew is concerned with the kingdom, Luke with the Jew–Gentile issue.

preceding the terrifying denunciations of Jerusalem, murderer of the prophets.[1]

Jerusalem treated them all the same—the old prophets, Jesus, the disciples of Jesus. There is a parallelism of action within St Luke's writings which is very significant. The resemblance of the Passion of St Stephen to that of Our Lord is particularly clear,[2] but everywhere we find a similar pattern: fidelity to Israel and the temple is followed by persecution from official Jewry, which in its turn results in the punishment of Jerusalem, the rejection of Israel and the proclamation of the mission to the Gentiles. This cycle in Our Lord's life, as depicted in the third gospel, has already been analysed; it is less obvious, but still clearly discoverable, in the early chapters of Acts relating to the general body of apostles. Their fidelity to the temple (Lk. 24:52–3; Acts 2:46–7, etc.) is rewarded by constant persecution (Acts 4:1–22; 5:17–40; 6:12–15, etc.) and this results in the scattering of the disciples abroad, and especially Philip's mission to Samaria and the baptism of the Ethiopian eunuch (Acts 8). But it is in the life of St Paul that the cycle of Our Lord's life is best reflected; this reflection is to be expected in so far as St Luke's theme was the same in his two books, and hence the central figures of the two may be expected—all proportions guarded—to resemble one another.

Both Jesus and Paul were a light to the Gentiles, not only

[1] For this reason the Lucan phrase 'and all the prophets' (13:28), absent from Matthew, is worth remarking; it helps to link the thought of verses 28–9 with that of verses 31–5.

[2] Of course this parallelism or resemblance is of the very essence of Christianity—the imitation of Christ, especially in the moral and spiritual order. Luke (in the case of Stephen almost certainly following a primitive Christian document) stresses also the external resemblances, as signs and proof of the internal, and as manifesting a certain pattern in history.

joined in function but actually by the very title (Lk. 2:32; Acts 13:47, Φῶς ἐθνῶν). Nevertheless, if when he is writing of Jesus and when he is writing of Paul Luke has a similar theological preoccupation uppermost in his mind, this does not mean that there is not a vast difference for him between the place of Jesus and the place of Paul in that theological scheme of things. Though Luke treats of them both, with special regard to the mystery of the rejection of the Jews and the calling of the Gentiles, their relation to this mystery is very different. Paul's life is subordinate to the mystery; it is something he preaches, something he witnesses to, but something which exists already, of which he is the servant. But the mystery itself is subordinate to Jesus' life and finds in the latter its very justification. Without the mystery of the calling of the Gentiles Paul's life would be meaningless, but without Jesus' life the very mystery of the calling of the Gentiles would lose its meaning. Jesus is the prophet-messiah, corner-stone of salvation; Paul is his witness.

We may consider Paul's life as related to the Lord's life in two ways: on the one hand, as sequel—Our Lord having been rejected by the Jews, it was for Paul to go to the Gentiles; one follows on the other: on the other hand, as the re-enactment—Christ having been rejected by the Jews, Paul, as a true other Christ, must also be rejected by the Jews; thus seen, it is not so much sequel as mirror. In fact this second aspect has been little considered and it is especially that which I wish to draw out here.

The story of Paul, like that of Jesus, begins with fidelity to the temple and the Law of Moses (cf., above all, Acts 22:1–5), and this fidelity always remained; his conversion to Christ never involved his turning away from the temple and the

synagogue. His constant visits to the synagogue are stressed
(Acts 13:14; 14:1; 17:1–17, etc.); he always preached first
to the Jews and only afterwards to the Gentiles, although he
was fully aware that his vocation was above all to the latter.
In this fidelity to the old order he was faithfully following
Jesus. His greatest period of activity—that of the chief missionary journeyings (Acts 15:30—21:15)—begins and ends at
Jerusalem; it was not for him, any more than it had been for
his master, to reject Jerusalem, but to be rejected by Jerusalem.
This is best seen in the narrative of his journey there. We have
seen how the central and most important part of the third
gospel treats of Jesus' journey to Jerusalem, a journey domi-
nated by the thought of the Passion which is to be its achievement. From the Transfiguration onwards Jesus is moving
towards Jerusalem and the death he is to meet there. There is
no hiding this death, on the contrary he prophesies it:

> Now we are going up to Jerusalem, and all that has been written
> by the prophets about the Son of Man is to be accomplished. He
> will be given up to the Gentiles, and mocked, and beaten, and
> spat upon; they will scourge him, and then they will kill him; but
> on the third day he will rise again (Lk. 18:31–3).

It is almost startling, on turning to the life of St Paul, to find
in the very centre of it a similar journey up to Jerusalem; and
not merely a journey to Jerusalem, but to his Passion in
Jerusalem. This is not now the journey of the prophet, but of
the witness: Paul goes up to Jerusalem to witness to Jesus by
word and suffering (20:24; 23:11). In the account of Paul's
life, Acts 19:21—'When all this was over, the thought in Paul's
heart was to go to Jerusalem'—has something of the same
significance as Luke 9:51 in the life of Our Lord. It is followed
by 20:16, 'He was eager, if he found it possible, to keep the

day of Pentecost at Jerusalem.' His eagerness reminds us of the same resolution of Jesus; and Paul, like Jesus, looked forward in Jerusalem to the passion and persecution which it always afforded the prophets of God. 'Now, a prisoner in spirit, I am going up to Jerusalem, knowing nothing of what is to befall me there; only, as I go on from city to city, the Holy Spirit assures me that at Jerusalem bondage and affliction await me' (20:22–3). He, like Jesus, has the guidance of the Spirit; but unlike Jesus, he has no full knowledge of the future. Moreover whereas it was Jesus who told His disciples of the coming Passion, Paul learns of it from the prophecies of others. The brethren at Tyre warned him not to go up to Jerusalem (Acts 21:4), and at Caesarea

> A prophet named Agabus came down from Judaea. When he visited us, he took up Paul's girdle, and bound his own hands and feet with it; then he said, Thus speaks the Holy Spirit, The man to whom this girdle belongs will be bound, like this, by the Jews at Jerusalem, and given over into the hands of the Gentiles. At hearing this, both we and our hosts implored Paul not to go up to Jerusalem. To which he answered, What do you mean by lamenting, and crushing my spirits? I am ready to meet prison and death as well in Jerusalem for the name of the Lord Jesus (Acts 21:10–13).

And so, we are told, he 'went up to Jerusalem' (21:15).[1] The Jews should have had no complaint to find with him; faithfully he went to the temple, publicly joining with four others in a week's purification. It was at this moment when

---

[1] St Luke's use of the two words Jerusalem and Hierosolyma in this journey-narrative is worth noting. Hierosolyma is used for all the bare statements of the journey—19:21; 21:4; 21:15; 21:17. Jerusalem is used for the two solemn prophecies of Paul's persecution in the city—20:22; 21:11–13. 20:16 is given as Hierosolyma by Westcott Hort and Merk, but as Jerusalem by Tischendorf.

Paul was most devout in the observances of the Old Law, in the service of the temple, that his passion in Jerusalem began. Attacked by the mob, dragged out of the temple, handed over to the Roman soldiers, tried before the Sanhedrin and then before the Roman governor, Paul bore his witness to Jesus in Jerusalem; and he bore witness especially by the very similarity between his treatment and that inflicted on his master. One high priest replaces another; Felix and Festus replace Pilate; Agrippa replaces Herod; but their functions in Christian history are to be compared. The following words addressed later by Paul to the Jews of Rome apply equally well to Jesus himself: 'Brethren, I am one who has done nothing to the prejudice of our people, or of our ancestral customs; yet, in Jerusalem, they handed me over to the Romans as a prisoner' (Acts 28:17). This handing over gave St Paul his opportunity to witness to Christ in the most solemn way. Jesus had told his disciples: 'Men will be laying hands on you and persecuting you; they will give you up to the synagogues, and to prison, and drag you into the presence of kings and governors on my account; that will be your opportunity to witness' (Lk. 21: 12–13). For this solemn witnessing in persecution, the Spirit's instruction was particularly promised (Lk. 12:11–12). Now St Paul is given this opportunity, and hence his long speeches before 'kings and governors' (chapters 24 and 26) have a special importance. They are in a way the culmination of Paul's career as witness. After such occasions there was really nowhere for him to go but to Caesar and Rome!

The Jews were not content simply to hand Paul over to the Gentiles; they sought his death as they had sought that of Jesus (23:12; 25:3), and Paul for his part was ready to meet death in Jerusalem for the name of Jesus (21:13); but this was not to be. In his own person the whole dramatic cycle had to be played out; not only his faithfulness to Israel and Israel's rejection of him, but also the full consequence of that rejection —Israel's own rejection made clear by the apostolate to the Gentiles. In prison in Jerusalem the Lord comes to his side and says to Paul, 'Do not lose heart; thou hast done with bearing me witness in Jerusalem, and now thou must carry the same witness to Rome' (23:11). And these words are made still clearer by others pronounced before, but still fresh in Paul's mind: uttered in the temple, they are the key to his vocation and his role in Christian history. 'Make haste, leave Jerusalem with all speed; they will not accept thy witness of me here. . . . Go, I mean to send thee afar off, to the Gentiles' (22: 18 21).

Paul is maltreated like Jesus and the prophets, and his re-action is the same. But whereas Jesus merely predicted the fall of Jerusalem and the universalization of the kingdom, it is Paul's mission actually to go forth to the Gentiles, 'to carry the same witness to Rome'. In order to bear this witness he has received the Holy Spirit and is possessed with a power (δύναμις) like that of Jesus (9:22; 19:11), which enables him to fulfil in his own person the whole programme of Acts 1:8. Similar to Jesus in his mission and treatment, carrying out the instructions left by Jesus to his disciples, it may seem strange that he was not given the character of the persecuted Jesus, the character of a prophet. It is true that Paul is numbered among the prophets in Acts 13:1 and he did prophesy his imminent Passion in Jerusalem; moreover in such incidents as his en-counter on Cyprus with Elymas the magician (a false prophet) Paul appears clearly as a true prophet filled with the Holy Spirit, and a miracle-worker (Acts 13:6–12). But, by and large, neither Luke nor Paul himself stresses Paul's prophetical character, though the idea was certainly present in the minds of both.[1] There are several reasons for this, the chief of which we already know: the function of the prophet was replaced by that of the apostle-witness, a change of name which indicates a change in the structure of God's Church on earth.[2] Prophets, named as such, remained in the Christian Church, and their function is not to be underestimated; but the name was acquiring a more specialized significance, and its bearer was subordinate to the apostle. The latter had become the really important title, and was the right one to give Paul, who indeed, in face of suggestions about his inferiority, found it necessary to stress his gift of apostleship very much indeed.[3]

With the title of apostle was intimately linked that of witness;

[1] Mgr Cerfaux also observes that 'it is remarkable that Paul never openly takes the title of prophet in the Old Testament sense. He is the servant of Christ, envoy of God, Christ's ambassador . . . . The success of the title of the apostle, to which St Paul contributed much, is in part explained by the necessity of marking clearly the originality of the Christian envoys. They have, unlike the prophets, a mission which is not personal to them and which does not wholly depend on their own revelation and visions: much as the philosophers were sent by Zeus to enlighten men in the name of reason, the apostles bear to the world, in God's name, the revelation of the Christ' (*Antinomie Paulinienne de la Vie Apostolique*, pp. 233–4). Of all the apostles Paul was the one with the most personal, the most 'prophetic' mission, but that remains the mission of a servant of Christ; and Paul's teaching remains the Gospel of Christ, it was not in the least personal to him as he was the first to recognize. There is no room for a Paul whose doctrine was personal to himself, culled from his own experience of conversion or from his visions (cf. Dodd, *According to the Scriptures*, p. 134).

[2] For a theological consideration of the difference between a prophetic and an apostolic economy see, for instance, P. Congar, O.P., *Vraie et Fausse Réforme dans l'Eglise*, pp. 78–80, 466–82.

[3] See 2 Cor. 12:11–12; 1 Cor. 9:1; 15:9–10; also the titles of many of the epistles.

St Paul himself attached great importance to it, to having *seen* the Lord and to having been appointed to proclaim what he had seen—'Am I not an apostle, have I not seen Our Lord Jesus Christ?' (1 Cor. 9:1). For Luke this was the most significant title of all: Acts is the history of witnessing. It is with Paul's right to the title of witness, to be indeed the supreme witness, that Luke concerns himself. 'Rise up and stand upon thy feet', says the Lord to Paul on the Damascus road, 'for to this end have I appeared to thee, that I may make thee a minister and a witness of those things which thou hast seen and of those things wherein I will appear to thee' (26:16). Ananias echoed the Lord's words in 22:15. Paul has not merely seen the Lord, he has been officially constituted witness of what he has seen, and this places him at least on a level with those to whom the original command of witnessing was given. His work frequently receives the name of witness,[1] and both its wide range and the unrivalled sufferings and persecutions which it brought on Paul made the title of witness one peculiarly his own.[2]

By his vision on the Damascus road and instant conversion, then, St Paul received the dual character of apostle and

[1] Acts 18:5; 20:21, 24; 23:11; 28:23.

[2] After their deaths Peter and Paul appear together as the two pre-eminent Christian witnesses, if we may interpret of them, as seems probable, Apoc. 11:3–12. And, what is worth noticing, these two witnesses are prophets: 'I will give the power of prophecy to my two witnesses.' The prophetical character of the two witnesses is very striking; but even more so is their assimilation to Christ. Like the Christ of St John (Jn. 18:37) they bear witness, and then they are killed. Their bodies lie in the streets of Sodom or Egypt, 'There too their Lord was crucified'. Like him they rise again after three days, and then ascend amid the clouds to heaven. St Luke's assimilation of Paul to Jesus is mild in comparison! But then St Luke was not writing a prophetical apocalypse but a study of historical theology.

witness.[1] Paul himself stressed his right to the first title, Luke to the second. If St Luke does not give Paul the name of apostle (apart from 14:4 and 13) it was perhaps so as to distinguish him clearly from the Twelve; it was certainly not to minimize the importance of this vessel of election. For him the title of witness was the most important, and its prophetical character brought Paul as close as was possible to Jesus the prophet, closer than if Paul had been given the now subsidiary title of prophet. In Luke's eyes Paul was witness because he had seen Christ, witness because he had fulfilled the Lord's command of witnessing throughout the whole world, witness because of his sufferings and trials before kings and governors. If in ecclesiastical tradition St Paul has received the astonishing title of 'The Apostle', for St Luke he was, quite simply, 'The Witness'.[2]

[1] St Stephen also is given the title of witness in 22:20; probably, like Paul, this was because of his vision of Jesus. But with Stephen the sense of the word is passing to its later and normal Christian meaning of martyr—one who, through persecution, has sealed his witness to Jesus with his life.

[2] The New Testament idea of witness, as we can now see, was most complex. At the risk of over-simplification I will point out here five differing, but interconnected, notions of the witness.

1. One who presents Christ and points him out (type: the Baptist).

2. One who gives evidence as to the fact of Christ's Resurrection (type: Peter).

3. One who knew Christ on earth (type: John the Evangelist).

4. One who preaches Christ to the world (type: Paul).

5. One who suffers and dies for Christ (type: Stephen).

No. 2 gives us the most primitive Christian idea of witness; 2, 4 and 5 are all Lucan, and all three contribute to his portrait of the witness Paul. 1, 3 and 5 are Johannine. For St Luke and St Paul the Holy Spirit is the supreme witness to Christ; while for St John and St Paul Jesus in his turn witnesses to the Father (1 Tim. 2:6–7; 6:13; Apoc. 1:5; 3:14).

9

AND SO ENTER INTO HIS GLORY

JESUS' death, his glorification and the universality of the
Church's subsequent mission are the three facts constituting
the irreducible core of Christian doctrine. The story of Christ
is that of the most glorious victory following on seeming de-
feat. On that victory the Church has been built, it is the
foundation of our faith and our apostolate: 'If Christ has not
risen, then our preaching is groundless' (1 Cor. 15:14). But
'the Lord has risen indeed'and this glorious Resurrection is the
key to the meaning of the Passion and all else. Jesus triumphed
as he was bound to, for 'Thou shalt not suffer thy holy one to
see corruption' (Ps.15:10), and therefore 'it was impossible that
death should have the mastery over him' (Acts 2:24). The
details of the Resurrection appearances may have a secondary
importance, but the fact of Jesus' glorification in soul and body
is absolutely primary. It is on account of his triumph over
death and sin that he is enthroned for ever as Lord and King;
through suffering he has entered into glory, and is now at the
right hand of God.[1] For the early Christians, centred as they
were on the essentials not the accidentals of their religion, it
was this that mattered most. It could be illustrated by one or

[1] Lk. 20:42; 22:69; Acts 2:34; 7:55.

other account of a post-Resurrection appearance; but these were told less for their own sake than as testimony to the supreme truth and as an inspiration to belief. There was less interest in recording an event simply for its intrinsic worth, and hence even an incident so striking to us as the Ascension could be almost passed over in the two first gospels. Jesus had risen, he had been seen by the appointed witnesses, he was now in heaven, both Christ and Lord. It was sufficient.

Naturally, however, the first primitive affirmation of their master's eminent glory was followed among Christians by a steady elaboration of teaching about this glory. If it was simple in its fullness, it also appeared complex in its manifestations. For instance, if there was glory already, there was far more to come: the post-Resurrection glory was still a partially veiled one. Again, even before the Resurrection, it was realized, there had been glory. And so, little by little, the theology of Jesus' glory grew, just as the whole of Christian theology grew, and the one seemed almost as extensive as the other.[1]

The theology of this glorification had a double root. One was the event of the Resurrection; the other was Jesus' earlier teaching about his second coming. During his life, apart from the last supper discourse as it is recorded by St John, Jesus had only spoken explicitly of his glory in connection with his second and final coming: 'If anyone is ashamed of acknowledging me and my words, the Son of man will be ashamed to acknowledge him, when he comes in his glory, with his Father and the holy angels to glorify him' (9:26). 'The very powers of heaven will rock. And then they will see the Son of man coming in a cloud,

---

[1] For the New Testament theology of glory see the admirable work, of which this chapter makes much use, by Doctor Ramsey, present Archbishop of York, *The Glory of God and the Transfiguration of Christ* (Longmans, 1949).

with great power and glory' (21:26–7). Notice also that it is as Son of man that Jesus is to receive glory. This was Our Lord's own favourite title, and the significance of it is important. There are still too many people who think that its point was simply to stress his perfect humanity. This is not so. Certainly it did present him as *the* man, new Adam, and it could at times help to suggest the depths of his suffering and humiliation: 'The Son of man has nowhere to lay his head' (9:58). But the point here remains precisely the contrast between the Son of man and the treatment he received, and in itself the title 'Son of man' suggests not lowliness but transcendence. When Jesus said that he was the Son of man, he had in mind the figure in the vision of the prophet Daniel, someone coming with power on the clouds of heaven. Hence Jesus' use of the title is a prime source for the theology of his glorification: the characteristics of the Son of man were power and glory. In his lifetime it was much more the power that was revealed; 'the Son of man has power to forgive sins' (5:24), and again, 'the Son of man has even the Sabbath at his disposal' (6:5)[1]; the glory still lay in the future, though the eye of faith could already perceive it and on certain occasions it was more evidently revealed. The key to the future lay in Jesus' combination of two Old Testament passages: Daniel 7 (the Son of man) and Psalm 109 (The Lord said to my lord, sit on my right hand). Together, they give us the ground for his supreme claim, 'A time is coming when the Son of man will be seated in power at God's right hand' (22:69), a claim made in all solemnity before the gathered Sanhedrin. This coming time was soon to arrive, for only a little later Stephen, standing in the same place, looked up and

---

[1] See A. Feuillet's illuminating study, 'L'Exousia du Fils de l'Homme', *Recherches de Science Religieuse* (1954), pp. 161–92.

saw 'heaven opening and the Son of man standing at the right hand of God' (Acts 7:55).

The glory of Jesus is that of his enthronement at the right hand of God, which was the sequel to the Resurrection and preliminary to the second coming; this whole cycle of glory being consequent upon Passion and death. Suffering is not an end; the suffering servant, Isaias had long ago proclaimed, was to be raised up and exalted (Is. 52:13). Through his pains, Jesus explained to his disciples on the Emmaus road, he had to enter into his glory, the glory of his kingship, revealed effectively to the apostles in the Resurrection appearances. There is an overwhelming impression of triumph and royalty in the gospel narratives of these events. First, angels in shining garments proclaim that it is useless to seek among the dead for the living one, and then Jesus himself appears to his disciples in the beauty of his risen body. Now there is no longer need to conceal his messiahship, he is clearly the Lord, enlightening minds, commanding the future 'unto all nations', promising 'power from on high' before ascending into heaven to God's right hand.

The Ascension is the link between the Resurrection and Jesus' abiding status in the heavens. It was so obvious that it hardly needed to be mentioned by the first evangelists, and consequently our detailed knowledge of it comes from the 'second generation' evangelist, St Luke. Jesus' presence on high at the right hand of his Father was the first of Christian mysteries; the visible event of the Ascension was the sacrament of this mystery. And there are several reasons why Luke may have wished to speak of it. First, it completed the cycle of the new Elias: Jesus like his predecessor ascended into the heavens leaving his power with the disciples who remained behind looking up as he went. Again it prepared the way for Pentecost and the early Church. St Luke's longer account of it appears in the book of Acts; this suggests that he saw the Ascension not so much as the end of Jesus' life on earth, but pre-eminently as the event preceding the descent of the Spirit. Jesus went up in order to send the Spirit down. Thirdly, his interest in the Ascension derives, I think, from his desire to emphasize the glory of Jesus as something that had already appeared. This glory was first spoken of as something to be experienced chiefly in the future, the awaited Parousia, but when the second coming proved less imminent than had at first been expected[1] it was natural to think more of what had already taken place. While awaiting Jesus' glorious descent from heaven, Christians could turn their minds to his already glorious ascent to heaven. Nevertheless the second coming was not by any means forgotten. On the contrary, the relationship between it and what has already taken place has always remained primary for the interpretation of every Christian mystery, all being at once past, present and future.

Christ will come, has come, is coming. This high mystery of the coming—so beautifully treated in the Advent liturgy—has sense in fact from every time angle. Nor do we speak of different, disconnected events, for one leads to another, opens the way to the next and prefigures that in which it will be fulfilled. Christ's first coming already establishes the kingdom on earth. It was present while he preached; for the Messiah was present, and that involved inevitably the presence also of the messianic age and the kingdom: already the blind had

---

[1] Luke 19:11 and 21:8 are generally cited as evidence that Luke himself did not think the Parousia imminent, but with how much force I do not know.

sight, and the prisoners went free, and the poor had the gospel preached to them. Yet the completion of the kingdom was still to come, the consequence of the triumphant Parousia. In the meantime an intermediate stage of the kingdom was reached with the Spirit's descent on the disciples. There is no room for a flat either/or, all the great mysteries of Christianity being at once eschatological, historical and ecclesiological. The Passion is the foreshadowing of the great tribulation of the latter days, the Resurrection of the final victory. Hence Jesus' glory was not only awaited as the last coming was awaited, but was also understood as already manifest in the Resurrection, and further in other events of Jesus' life. The more Christians thought, the more they realized that, hidden though it might be, Jesus' glory had never been absent. It derived not only from his historical triumph on the cross and over the empty tomb, but also from his nature of Son of God. His ontological glory was with him from the start when the angels had sung above the stable of his birth, and it remained through the whole ministry till the great climax. St Luke speaks much more of this glory than did the first evangelists and the Transfiguration especially became for him a manifestation of Jesus' abiding glory at the same time as a prefiguration of Resurrection and Parousia. St John went further still, and the fourth gospel shows the whole life of Jesus bathed in a hardly veiled light of glory; here passion and glorification have come to overlap. John points out the glory of the cross itself, an idea which has always persisted in Christian thought, side by side with the other one of the utter emptying of the crucified Jesus, the Kenosis. In this matter as elsewhere St Luke stands somewhat between the first gospels and the fourth.

Certainly in Luke, as everywhere in Christian teaching, one

finds the great cycle of suffering, rejection, death and the exaltation of victory. This cycle exists already in Isaias 53 which was applied at once to the interpretation of Jesus' life, while the classical statement of the whole drama is Philippians 2:6–11, most tremendous of Christological hymns. The basic elements of the cycle can never change, but a variation of stress is to be found even in the canonical writings. At first the suffering was felt most keenly, in the early period of 'Petrine' theology. Later the suffering came to be a little passed over in the leap of triumphant joy in the victory of Christ, and the cross itself was transformed into an eschatological sign of victory. If Christ's glory came to be more and more central within the realm of Christian thought, it was not interpreted identically by all. While Matthew and Mark had placed the manifest glory of Christ chiefly in the second coming, St Paul delighted more in his cosmological glory, and St John stressed the glory apparent all through Jesus' life and Passion; St Luke, for his part, centred his doctrine on the trio of Transfiguration, Resurrection and Ascension.

> The fashion of his face was altered, and his garments became white and dazzling; and two men appeared conversing with him, Moses and Elias, seen now in glory; and they spoke of the death which he was to achieve at Jerusalem. Meanwhile Peter and his companions were sunk in sleep; and they awoke to see him in his glory (9:29–32).

On the holy mountain the transcendence of Jesus was most clearly revealed; here the glory which was his by right of nature and which would shine out clearly with a new title from the triumph of the Resurrection was for a moment beheld by the bewildered eyes of the chosen apostles. It was Jesus' own glory: 'his glory' is a phrase dear to St Luke, he uses it three times,[1] for instance where St Mark wrote 'when he comes in his Father's glory with the holy angels' (Mk. 8:38), St Luke puts 'when he comes in his own glory and that of the Father and of the holy angels' (9:26). The glory of the Transfiguration is linked with his coming departure from this world in Jerusalem, about which Jesus conversed with Moses and Elias, and it points to the greater glory of the last coming of which Jesus had already spoken. Prior to that last coming these three events of Transfiguration, Resurrection, Ascension formed a growing crescendo of majesty. In each there is the same vision of brightness and splendour: garments, white and dazzling. And in each there is the appearance of two men—'And behold two men', exactly the same phrase being used by St Luke on each occasion to introduce them.[2] Evidently this repetition is intended to connect the three occasions together, following each other in the manifestation of the glory of the Lord. The repetition is the more striking as in fact they were not men but angels in the two later events.

The Ascension took place on Mount Olivet (Acts 1:12), and the site of the last mystery of Jesus' earthly life is well worth noting. If Mount Olivet witnessed his greatest triumph, his bearing up in glory, the same mountain had already seen his deep affliction, the night of anguish preceding the Passion (Lk. 22:39). For St Luke the most bitter of all the moments of Jesus' suffering was this vigil of prayer in the garden when

> he parted from them, going a stone's throw off, and knelt down to pray; Father, he said, if it pleases thee, take away this chalice

[1] Lk. 9:26; 9:32; 24:26.

[2] καὶ ἰδοὺ ἄνδρες δύο. Lk. 9:30; 24:4; Acts 1:10. This repetition is noted by C. P. Jones, 'The Epistle to the Hebrews and the Lucan Writings', in *Studies in the Gospels* (Blackwell, 1955), p. 126.

from before me; only as thy will is, not as mine is. And he had sight of an angel from heaven, encouraging him. And now he was in agony, and prayed still more earnestly; his sweat fell to the ground like thick drops of blood (Lk. 22:41-4).[1]

St Luke is the only evangelist to mention the apparition of the angel and the sweat of blood. The agony and the Ascension are the two extremes in Jesus' story as described by Luke, for even on Calvary Jesus is not humiliated so utterly as in the garden. Both occur on Mount Olivet; this links together Jesus' going down and his rising up, his suffering with his glory.

In both scenes on Mount Olivet not only was Jesus present but also the apostles and angels. The first angel had the mission to encourage Jesus himself, while after the Ascension the angels are concerned with encouraging the apostles, who had previously been left to sleep undisturbed. Just as after the Ascension the Holy Spirit of Jesus is given to the apostles, so also is his angelic protection and encouragement. In every way the economy of Christian life within the Church is the transfer to the ordinary disciple of the earthly life of Our Lord himself.

Whereas in the Old Testament the glory of God was revealed in the temple of Jerusalem,[2] it is now revealed in the person of Jesus. Here again we see how Jesus has taken the place of the temple. He is the new centre of the world, the place from which the divine glory now radiates. It was because of this profound replacing that Jesus could speak of his body

---

[1] The two verses referring to the agony, the angel, and the sweat of blood do not appear in the Vatican codex, nor in some other early versions of the New Testament. However, their authenticity is quite well supported in other versions and writers (e.g. Justin, Irenaeus and Tatian), and it is much easier to explain their omission (as inconsistent with Christ's dignity) than their addition.

[2] 3 Kings 8:11; Is. 6:1-3; 60:1; Ez. 10:4; 44:4.

while the Jews thought he was referring to the temple (Jn. 2:19–21). They were as preoccupied with the latter as Christians are with Christ, and for them the unforgivable sin was Jesus' claim to be greater than the house of God (Mt. 12:6).

If Jesus can be glorified it is because he is the Lord. This title which became so normal among Christians in speaking of Jesus is typically Lucan. In his lifetime he was most probably called 'Lord' only at moments of messianic triumph such as the entry into Jerusalem,[1] the disciples' normal name for him being 'Master'. The two first synoptic writers do not use the title of 'Lord' in their own narrative, and St John only does so rarely; but St Luke makes frequent use of it, fourteen times in all. Perhaps this is a sign of St Paul's influence.

Luke's is a kingly gospel. Jesus is Lord because he is the messianic king of all ages and all lands. 'The Lord God will give him the throne of his father David, and he shall reign over the house of Jacob eternally; his kingdom shall never have an end' (1:32–3). 'As my Father has allotted a kingdom to me', Jesus said to his disciples during the last supper, 'so I allot to you a place to eat and drink at my table in my kingdom' (22:29). It was as king that he was received in Jerusalem—'Blessed is the king, they said, who comes in the name of the Lord; peace and glory in heaven above' (19:38). Luke's messianic doctrine is both royal and prophetical. St Irenaeus described St Luke's as the 'priestly gospel', but this really seems far from the mark. Jesus' priestly function and his fulfilment of the Old Testament priesthood are hardly noticed in the third gospel. Here he is not high priest but prophet and king. The crowds who welcomed him to Jerusalem probably thought him a new king of the Jews in a very earthly sense, the nationalist monarch of a

[1] See Cerfaux's article 'Kyrios' in the *Dictionnaire de la Bible*, Supplément.

jealous race. Too many of his friends hoped for that sort of a messiah, and the fears of his enemies as well were formulated in such terms. Not forgetting his recent state entry into Jerusalem, the chief priests accused him to Pilate of plotting for a crown. 'We have discovered, they said, that this man is subverting the loyalty of our people, forbids the payment of tribute to Caesar, and calls himself Christ the king. And Pilate asked him, Art thou the king of the Jews?' (23:2–3). Therefore over the cross was the proclamation written 'This is the King of the Jews' (23:38)—a joke, no doubt, but too close to the truth even in their eyes to please the Jewish leaders. Yet Jesus' claim was quite other than they had imagined, and their actions merely hastened the coming of his kingdom: not only over the Jews, but over all peoples and lands. The disciples had been wrong if they thought that the kingdom would begin that day at the descent of Mount Olivet, or be centred on Jerusalem. Jesus had already taught them otherwise in parable.

> He went on and told them a parable; this was because he had now nearly reached Jerusalem, and they supposed that the kingdom of God was to appear immediately. He told them, then, there was a man of noble birth, who went away to a distant country, to have the royal title bestowed upon him, and so return (19:11–12).

The parable is admittedly obscure, but it links up the kingdom with a distant land and a time not the present. 'Others will come from the east and the west, the north and the south, to take their ease in the kingdom of God' (13:29).

Jesus is king of the new world-embracing and eternal realm, yet high as is such dignity it does not exhaust the meaning of his Lordship. He is Lord because he is God. The title had always been pre-eminently though not uniquely divine, and its New Testament use embraced most assuredly its fullest meaning. The Son is not less than his Father, and the same title on Elizabeth's lips can be given to the two within one conversation. 'The message that was brought to thee from the Lord shall have fulfilment' (1:45) and 'How have I deserved to be thus visited by the mother of my Lord?' (1:43). Jesus is the Christ whom the Lord had anointed (2:26), but he is also himself the Lord Christ, the Saviour (2:11).

His life on earth leads up, for Luke, to the last great moment of glory on the mountain which is called Olivet. To that event all was leading from the time in Galilee when Jesus turned his eyes steadfastly towards Jerusalem, for 'the time was drawing near for his assumption' (9:51). This lifting up was the completion of the exodus of which he had spoken with the prophets on the mountain, at one and the same time victorious departure from this world and glorious entry into the heavenly sphere. 'They saw him lifted up, and a cloud caught him away from their sight' (Acts 1:9). That was Luke's picture of the end of Jesus' past earthly life and achievement, but not the completion of all, not the final glory. That was, and is, still to come. 'Men of Galilee, why do you stand here looking heavenwards? He who has been taken from you into heaven, this same Jesus, will come back in the same fashion, just as you have watched him going into heaven' (Acts 1:11). The Ascension is no substitute but a pledge of the second coming. Only then will Jesus fully 'enter into his glory'. It may be far off, it may be necessary first to travel into many distant lands, to suffer much persecution and tribulation, but the second coming remains as certain as the first, guaranteed by the Ascension.

Yes, much has to be done first; the Holy Spirit above all has to prepare the way: when the disciples asked yet again about the imminence of the kingdom, Jesus answered them: 'Enough for you, that the Holy Spirit will come upon you, and you will receive strength from him' (Acts 1:8); with that strength Christians have to acknowledge the Son of Man, and so prepare themselves to be acknowledged by him (Lk. 9:26); they must keep themselves ever waiting and watching, clinging to their faith even when all hope seems gone and the power of the world is turned against them, for only then will their Lord come (12:36–8; 18:8).

> The sun and the moon and the stars will give portents, and on earth the nations will be in distress, bewildered by the roaring of the sea and of its waves; men's hearts will be dried up with fear, as they await the troubles that are overtaking the whole world; the very powers of heaven will rock. And then they will see the Son of Man coming in a cloud, with his full power and majesty (21:25–7).

As Resurrection followed Passion, the Parousia will follow the world tribulation of the latter days. The whole world will share in the Passion of Jesus that it may share also in his glory. Finally, the promise of the angels will be fulfilled: the time of watching over, the new age will begin when the Lord Jesus Christ appears with power and glory on the clouds of heaven by the right hand of his Father, and in lowly fear and ardent love men at last witness the return of the King.

10

SALVATION IS NOT TO BE FOUND ELSEWHERE

In chapter four of the Acts there is an account of a speech of St Peter before a gathering of the chief priests and elders of the Jews. Peter and John had been arrested for healing a lame man at the Beautiful Gate of the temple and making use of the occasion to address a crowd in Solomon's Porch. In his defence before the chief priests, Peter went quickly to the point:

> You crucified Jesus Christ, the Nazarene, and God raised him from the dead; it is through his name that this man stands before you restored. He is that stone, rejected by you, the builders, that has become the chief stone at the corner. Salvation is not to be found elsewhere; this alone of all the names under heaven has been appointed to men as the one by which we must needs be saved (Acts 4:10–12).

In this speech, after stating the facts of Crucifixion and Resurrection, Peter interprets them by means of the Old Testament text which we already know so well; his use of it here is a reminder that it became at once a fundamental passage for early Christian theology.[1] It could be used to illustrate the chief theme of this book. 'Jesus Christ, the Nazarene' was

[1] Made use of not only here and in Luke 20:17 and parallel places, but also in Romans 9:33 and 1 Peter 2:7.

the subject of chapters 5 and 6; 'that stone, rejected by you the builders', chapter 7; while the phrase 'has become the chief stone at the corner' might sum up the argument of chapters 8 and 9. St Peter's final comment remains for the present chapter: 'Salvation is not to be found elsewhere.' The gospel that Peter and Paul and the whole Church preached was the good news of salvation, and salvation through Jesus. As the idea of salvation is very much to the fore in St Luke's work, and as it gives point to everything else, it is well to end with it: for St Luke, as for the Creed, the explanation of Jesus' life and death lies here—it was all *'propter nos, et nostram salutem'*. This salvation comes from Jesus; he is the salvation of God, and it is in his name, and in it only, that sins may be forgiven, the gospel preached, new life offered to men. 'This alone of all the names under heaven has been appointed to men as the one by which we must needs be saved' (Acts 4:12). 'It was fitting that Christ should suffer, and should rise again from the dead on the third day; and that repentance and remission of sins should be preached in his name to all nations, beginning at Jerusalem' (Lk. 24:46–7). The gospel of merciful salvation is the burden of Luke's writing from end to end; repentance and the forgiveness of sins through faith in Jesus is its central theme. At the beginning Simeon takes Jesus in his arms and prophesies that his eyes have seen the salvation of God prepared for all nations, and at the end Paul declares to the Jews of Rome that the message of salvation has been sent by God to the nations, and they at least will not reject it (Lk. 2:30; Acts 28:28); already in the mouth of Zachary (Lk. 1:77) this salvation means the forgiveness of sins; the call to repentance and forgiveness is the message of his son John preparing men for the approaching moment when they are 'to see the salvation of God'; it is the primary note of the kingdom in Jesus' preaching, and it is the constant theme of the apostles who followed him.[1]

The prime activity of the apostles was to witness to the Resurrection as proof that Jesus was the Messiah sent by God to redeem his people. This witnessing was destined to produce faith and repentance in its hearers, and those who thus accepted the gospel of salvation had their sins forgiven in the name of Jesus and by the power of the Spirit. So on one occasion Peter told the high priests that God 'has raised him [Jesus] up to his right hand, as the prince and saviour who is to bring Israel repentance, and remission of sins. Of this, we are witnesses; we and the Holy Spirit God gives to all those who obey him' (Acts 5:31–2), or again he told Cornelius that 'all the prophets bear him [Jesus] this testimony, that everyone who has faith in him is to find remission of sins through his name' (Acts 10:43). This remark followed immediately after an affirmation of the Crucifixion and Resurrection, and St Paul drew exactly the same practical conclusion from his preaching of the Passion and Resurrection at Pisidian Antioch: 'Here is news for you, then, brethren; remission of your sins is offered to you through him. There are claims from which you could not be acquitted by the law of Moses, and whoever believes in Jesus is quit of all these' (Acts 13:38–9). The Resurrection and glorification of Jesus was not seen as the end but rather as the means whereby the saviour of the world has brought salvation to all men who will turn from their sins to faith in his name.[2]

[1] Lk. 3:3–8; 5:20, 32; 7:48; 19:7–10. Acts 2:38; 3:19, 26; 10:43; 13:38; etc.

[2] For the other side of things we have to look rather to the Pauline epistles, for instance Ephesians 1:3–14, where the forgiveness of sins and the gospel of salvation appear as means to the complete glorification of Christ.

Salvation through faith in Jesus is not a purely inward conversion, but a total and manifest change of life. Hence its condition is a visible rite—baptism, at once the sacrament of repentance and of incorporation into the Church, given to those who believe in Jesus.

> And the eunuch said, See, there is water here; why may I not be baptised? Philip said, if thou dost believe with all thy heart, thou mayest. And he answered, I believe that Jesus Christ is the Son of God. So he had the chariot stopped, and both of them, Philip and the eunuch, went down into the water, and Philip baptised him there (Acts 8:36–8).

Baptism is the visible and efficacious sign of faith, salvation, repentance and the forgiveness of sins. 'Repent, Peter said to them, and be baptised, every one of you, in the name of Jesus Christ, to have your sins forgiven' (Acts 2:38). So if repentance and forgiveness of sins through the name of Jesus is the gospel which the apostles have to preach throughout the whole world, it is baptism in the name of Jesus which is the means whereby the repentant receive this forgiveness. The relation of this baptism to that of John was clearly a problem for some,[1] as John's was also a 'baptism whereby men repented to have their sins forgiven' (Lk. 3:3). But that forgiveness is now given 'in the name of Jesus Christ': this in fact is the point—the forgiveness offered by Peter to the assembled people at Pentecost derived immediately from the events about which he had just spoken to them, the Passion and Resurrection of Jesus and the consequent bestowal of the Holy Spirit. The new baptism is not only a baptism of forgiveness but also one of the Spirit, dependent on the death of Jesus; hence St Paul could say,

[1] Thus instruction in 'the different types of baptism' had to be given to neophytes, Hebrews 6:2.

appealing to the common knowledge of his readers, 'You know well enough that we who were taken up into Christ by baptism have been taken up, all of us, into his death' (Rom. 6:3), and St Peter, having told his hearers to be baptized, could continue, 'then you will receive the gift of the Holy Spirit' (Acts 2:38); hence, too, John the Baptist had prophesied that Jesus would 'baptize you with the Holy Ghost and with fire' (Lk.3:16) and Jesus himself before the Ascension had promised the apostles 'a baptism with the Holy Spirit' which he contrasted with 'John's baptism with water' (Acts 1:5, compare 11:16).

If Christian baptism is baptism into the death of Jesus, Jesus' death was itself a baptism: 'There is a baptism I must needs be baptised with, and how impatient am I for its accomplishment!' (Lk. 12:50). This again links Jesus' death with its prefiguration —his own messianic baptism in the Jordan when he went down into the waters of death and came up to receive the Holy Spirit descending upon him (Lk. 3:22); and as the Spirit's descent upon Jesus followed his baptism in the Jordan so the Spirit's baptismal descent upon Jesus' disciples follows his baptism of death. Without this link it would be difficult to explain the importance that Jesus' baptism had for the early Church. But once it is understood, we see how much more our Spirit baptism produces than forgiveness of sins—it gives us the whole life dependent upon Christ's death and Resurrection and symbolized in the events of his Jordan baptism—a sharing of his Spirit, and sonship of his Father within the fold of his Church. The Father is Jesus' Father, and He becomes ours in so far as we are Jesus' disciples and members of his kingdom. 'Do not be afraid, you, my little flock. Your Father has determined to give you his kingdom' (Lk. 12:32) and this kingdom is given to the disciples precisely through the gift of the Spirit (Acts 1:6–8) in baptism.

The immediate consequence of baptism was entry into the Church, the community of those faithful to the name of Jesus and guided by his Spirit. The Church is the new Israel, taking the place of Jerusalem and the old Israel rejected for their infidelity; or, rather, she is the faithful remnant of the first Israel which has survived, as the prophets foretold, scattered among the peoples. In chapter 6 we saw how the Church received her founder's character—the guidance of the Spirit, constancy in prayer, prophetic inspiration. In these qualities she was faithful to her master, but faithful also to her position as the new Israel, successor to the old. The first Israel, shown to us in chapters 1 and 2 of the third gospel, had the same characteristics; doubtless the unprecedented outburst of spiritual and prophetic activity there recorded could be explained only as the sign of the Messiah's coming; nevertheless it took place within the community of those faithful to the old Israel and was fully in keeping with her character. This character now passed from her, through Jesus, to the new Israel, the Church. Within this Church dwelt the Spirit-led disciples of Jesus. They shared a common life, which is nowhere better described than in the few words Luke used to sum up the effect of Peter's Pentecostal exhortation: 'All those who had taken his words to heart were baptised, and about three thousand souls were won for the Lord that day. These occupied themselves continually with the apostles' teaching, their fellowship in the breaking of bread and the fixed times of prayer' (Acts 2:41–2). The Christian Church was a fellowship, entered into by baptism, controlled by the apostolic preaching, manifested in the breaking of bread and in prayer. It was a

11

fellowship, a spiritual communion (κοινωνία); this is a key word for the understanding of early Christian life and for St Paul's thought, but it is the only time St Luke uses it. Christian life is a sharing with God, with Christ, with one another—a sharing of the Spirit, of the body of Christ, of material possessions. 'There was one heart and soul in all the company of believers; none of them called any of his possessions his own, everything was shared in common' (4:32). It was a fellowship pre-eminently in the Spirit, but manifested in the flesh, in earthly goods: 'All those who owned farms or houses used to sell them, and bring the price of what they had sold to lay it at the apostles' feet, so that each could have what share of it he needed' (4:34–5). Thus within the Church of Jerusalem they could provide for the widows and the needy, as later the Gentile churches provided for the needy Church of Jerusalem herself (11:29; 24:17).

This fellowship was guaranteed by unity of faith in Christ through 'the apostles' teaching', for this society full of the spirit of brotherhood and of spontaneous sharing yet had its hierarchy—the Twelve, and others chosen in subordination to them: the presbyters and deacons on whom hands had been laid. The Church was a society where freedom grew up with authority, both being gifts of one Spirit. She had begun with that first group of the hundred and twenty centred on 'Peter and John, James and Andrew, Philip and Thomas, Bartholomew and Matthew, James the son of Alphaeus and Simon the Zealot, and Judas the brother of James' (1:13). All Christians witnessed to Christ, but primarily the apostles; all received the Spirit, but pre-eminently the apostles. The apostles were able to speak in the name of the Spirit (5:1–3), and the failure of Ananias and Sapphira to lay all the money at the apostles' feet was not merely to deceive them but to defraud the Spirit. So close was this union with the Spirit that 'We and the Holy Spirit' could become an apostolic formula (5:32; 15:28). The Twelve stood at the heart of the Church, and at the centre of the Twelve stood Peter. His unique position was given him by Jesus and no other: 'I have prayed for thee, that thy faith may not fail; when, after a while, thou hast come back to me, it is for thee to be the support of thy brethren' (Lk. 22:32). He was the 'support of his brethren', and he became so even before the Ascension. His authority already guaranteed the Resurrection—'The Lord has indeed risen, and has appeared to Simon' (Lk. 24:34). Afterwards he takes the initiative with a sense of assurance. 'Peter stood up and spoke before all the brethren' (Acts 1:15), and a new apostle was appointed. It is he who addresses the crowds and the Sanhedrin, he who works miracles in the name of Jesus Christ, he who suffers in prison. Luke is careful to point out that Peter was not only the apostle for the circumcised, but also of the Gentiles: 'Brethren, you know well enough how from early days it has been God's choice that the Gentiles should hear the message of the gospel from my lips, and so learn to believe' (15:7). It was through Peter that, in the person of Cornelius, the first Gentile had been baptized. Luke could afterwards concern himself exclusively with the Gentile missions of Paul, but no careful reader would conclude from this that the movement of the apostolate from Jerusalem to the pagan world meant the superseding of St Peter. He was and remained the 'support of his brethren', of St Paul no less than of the others, for the justification of Paul's works could be found in Peter's words in the assembly at Jerusalem.

Just as the fellowship of the Church was entered into by the sacrament of baptism, so its life was centred around 'the breaking of bread'. It was the most moving of moments, inserted within the traditional Jewish rite, at once prayer and meal, when an apostle or presbyter taking bread in his hands as Jesus had taken it at that last unforgettable supper before his Passion 'blessed and broke it, and gave it to them, saying, This is my body, given for you . . . , And so with the cup, when supper was ended, This cup, he said, is the new testament in my blood which is to be shed for you' (Lk. 22:19–20). Jesus had done it, and what he had done he commanded that his disciples should do, a memorial of his dying for them, of the sacrifice of this new alliance: 'Do this for a commemoration of me.' It was the commemoration at once of Jesus' last supper, his death, and above all of his Resurrection: that was why it was held on the first day of the week. The early Christians gathered together on the day of the Resurrection to break bread in the house of one or another of their company, and the sacramental commemoration of Jesus' death and Resurrection became the centre of the new liturgy. Dispersed from Jerusalem, little communities scattered in the great Gentile world, their members came together for the Sunday communion: prayer, reading, and the act of thanksgiving. Gatherings like that of Troas, when Paul was there, were the very soul of the new Christian life. 'When the new week began, we had met for the breaking of bread, and Paul was preaching to them; he meant to leave them next day, and he continued speaking till midnight. . . . And so he broke bread and ate; afterwards he talked with them for some time until dawn came, when he left' (Acts 20:7, 11). Luke's linking of the Christian fellowship (κοινωνία) with the breaking of bread (2:42) was not for-tuitous. From their union at the one table came the union of

Christians in their whole common life. 'The bread, that we break, is it not a sharing (κοινωνία) in the body of the Lord?' (1 Cor. 10:16).

With the Eucharistic breaking of bread was joined prayer, at first in the temple and the synagogues, but then as the gap between the Old Israel and the New became ever wider, increasingly in the private houses of Christians. With it was often united fasting, and at these times of fast and prayer the Holy Spirit was especially close to his own. At Jerusalem 'When they had finished praying, they were all filled with the Holy Spirit' (4:31), while at Antioch 'The Church had as its prophets and teachers Barnabas, and Simon who was called Niger, and Lucius of Cyrene, and Manahen, foster-brother of Herod the tetrarch, and Saul. These were offering worship to God and fasting[1] when the Holy Spirit said, I must have Barnabas and Saul dedicated to the work to which I have called them. Thereupon they fasted and prayed and laid their hands on them, and so took leave of them. And they, sent on their travels by the Holy Spirit, went down to Seleucia' (13:1–4). The Spirit was the unifying principle in Church life: in the primary gifts of faith and repentance, and the subsequent life of prayer and action, apostolate and prophecy, in persecution and the working of miracles, in witnessing and speaking with tongues, it was always the same Spirit—that 'Holy Spirit God gives to all those who obey him' (5:32), the very 'Spirit of Jesus' (16:7).

Among other characteristics of the new Christian order, we may consider that of peace. 'Peace on earth' was what

[1] The meaning of this difficult phrase is examined by Erik Peterson, 'La λειτουργία des Prophètes et des Didascales a Antioche', *Recherches de Science Religieuse* (1949), pp. 577–9. There were not two activities, it seems, but one, the λειτουργία being itself a fast. The meaning is that while certain people were observing a fast at Antioch, the Holy Spirit spoke to them.

the angels promised the shepherds on Christmas night, and 'the way of peace' was what Zachary prophesied would be the fruit of Jesus' coming (Lk. 2:14; 1:79). Jesus on his triumphal entry into Jerusalem was hailed as one bringing peace (19:38) and Peter told Cornelius that it is news of peace which God has sent to Israel through Jesus Christ (Acts 10:36). Yet Jesus prophesied persecution not tranquillity for his disciples, and conflict with those who refused to acknowledge him: 'Do you think that I have come to bring peace on the earth? No, believe me, I have come to bring dissension' (Luke 12:51). Hence it is a record of constant persecution which Luke gives us in Acts. Clearly the peace which Jesus had come to give was not the world's kind; it was that inner spirit of joy which no persecution could diminish. Joy is for Luke the natural concomitant to the gifts of faith and repentance. 'The Gentiles were rejoiced to hear this, and praised the word of the Lord, and they found faith' (Acts 13:48). Joy, not sorrow, was the apostles' reaction to Jesus' departure at the Ascension, and it remained a constant characteristic of the Christian life (Lk. 24:52; Acts 2:46). Its presence was especially noticeable in times of persecution (Acts 5:41) and this appears natural when we see that it was closely connected with the Spirit's presence both in Jesus and in his disciples (Lk. 10:21; Acts 13:52), and remember as well that the Spirit was to be present to the disciples above all in time of persecution (Lk. 12:11–12). Hence joy in persecution follows of itself. Those were times of especial blessedness:

> Blessed are you, when men hate you and cast you off and revile you, when they reject your name as something evil, for the Son of Man's sake. When that day comes, rejoice and exult over it; for behold, a rich reward awaits you in heaven; their fathers treated

the prophets no better. . . . Woe upon you, when all men speak well of you; their fathers treated the false prophets no worse (Lk. 6:22–3, 26).

Persecution was to be the continual lot of the Christian community (see also Lk. 21:12–18) and a thing full of fruitfulness: it is a reason for exultation, an opportunity for witnessing, an occasion of prophecy. Moreover this beatitude puts the persecuted Church, like Jesus himself, within the perspective of the prophets of old: heirs of the prophets, Christians, like their master, can expect only the treatment of a prophet. Thus the Holy Spirit's presence, persecution, joy, and the Church's prophetic character went hand in hand, and were all marks of the true disciples of Jesus.

Another and fundamental mark was poverty. If there is one basic virtue or characteristic of the blessed in the thought of St Luke, it is to be poor, materially poor. It is the profound meaning of the beatitudes, as he records them.[1] 'Blessed are you who are poor, the kingdom of God is yours' (Lk. 6:20). Luke's change in the form of these sayings, from the third to the second person, gives them a particularly ecclesiological character: the disciples themselves are addressed by Jesus, and their title to blessedness is proclaimed. It is merit to be poor, as it is near-condemnation to be rich. The first beatitude and its attendant curse—'Woe upon you who are rich; you have your comfort already' (Lk. 6:24)—find their practical application in the parable of Dives and Lazarus. 'There was a rich man once, that was clothed in purple and lawn, and feasted sumptuously every day. And there was a beggar, called Lazarus, who lay at his gate, covered with sores,

[1] See the fine study by Dom Dupont, *Les Béatitudes* (Louvain, 1954), pp. 183–244; of this I have made very much use.

wishing that he could be fed with the crumbs which fell from the rich man's table, but none was ready to give them to him; the very dogs came and licked his sores' (Lk. 16:19-21). Luke is fond of these sharp contrasts—Blessed are you, woe upon you—rich and poor, pharisees and publicans, Jews and Gentiles. Dives was not a bad man, only a rich one who used his riches to gain earthly happiness. Again, Luke does not tell us of Lazarus' virtue, only of his poverty; yet he dies, and is carried to Abraham's bosom: he is the blessed poor one, 'the kingdom of God is yours'. And the rich man? He found his grave in hell. Why? Because he had had his fortune on earth, he had nothing more to come to him: 'Woe upon you who are rich; you have your comfort already.' On earth Lazarus had only discomfort; in heaven the roles are reversed. This reversal is typical of Luke's moral teaching: 'Abraham said, My Son, remember that thou didst receive thy good fortune in thy lifetime, and Lazarus, no less, his ill-fortune; now he is in comfort, thou in torment' (16:25). The other beatitudes are only confirmation of this principle. 'Blessed are you who are hungry now; you will have your fill' (6:21), Lazarus the hungry one is now fed. 'Woe upon you who are filled full; you shall be hungry' (6:25), good eating is the mark of the rich man: 'Come, soul, thou hast goods in plenty laid up for many years to come; take thy rest now, eat, drink, and make merry' (12:19). It is all cut short, the rich man dies—'this night thou must render up thy soul'—and is buried in hell and, begging only for a drop of water, it is refused him.

This is without any doubt a basic element in Christian teaching—the complete upturning of this world's order of things. The rich and the well-fed and the well-spoken of, all those blessed with the goods of this world, come indeed into a very sorry plight, while all the unfortunate are loaded with the true blessings. It is the consequence of the coming of Jesus, 'Sign of contradiction'. God 'has put down the mighty from their seats, and exalted the lowly; he has filled the hungry with good things, and sent the rich away empty-handed' (1:52–3). If this is common Christian teaching, it was an idea particularly dear to St Luke. He was constantly returning to it, and he stressed the character of the first Christian community as a fellowship of the poor, of people who made a really good use of what they had. That was the fault of Dives, he simply feasted, spent his money on earth and not on heaven. 'My counsel to you is, make use of your base wealth to win yourselves friends, who, when you leave it behind, will welcome you into eternal habitations' (16:9). That is just what the rich man did not do, 'Thou fool, this night thou must render up thy soul; and who will be master of all thou hast laid up? Thus it is with the man who lays up treasure for himself, and has no credit with God' (12:20–1).

If we have riches we must use them for the other world and for others. At the very least a radical generosity is required: 'When thou givest hospitality, invite poor men to come, the cripples, the lame, the blind: so thou shalt win a blessing, for these cannot make thee any return; thy reward will come when the just shall rise again' (14:13–14). Zacchaeus was saved, but only by a drastic treatment of his possessions: 'Here and now, Lord, I give half of what I have to the poor; and if I have wronged anyone in any way, I make restitution of it fourfold' (19:8). Even better, however, was to give not half but all, to leave all that one has and follow Jesus. It was the way, not obligatory but encouraged, of the early Church: 'All those who owned farms or houses used to sell them, and bring the price of what they had sold to lay it at the apostles' feet, so that each could have what share of it he needed' (Acts 4:34–5). What Luke continually stressed was the completeness of the renunciation of one's goods which was required; this is most striking. In Mark we read that Jesus told the rich young man to 'sell what belongs to thee; give it to the poor, and so the treasure thou hast shall be in heaven'; Luke follows Mark's text but adds the one word 'all' (πάντα): 'Sell all that belongs to thee'.[1] Exactly the same addition is to be found in Luke's accounts of the calling of the first apostles and of Levi; where Mark says of the latter 'he rose up and followed Jesus', Luke writes 'he rose up, and left all behind, and followed him' (Mk. 2:14; Lk. 5:28). Luke insists on complete renouncement; his is an exacting gospel: 'None of you can be my disciple, if he does not take leave of all that he possesses' (14:33). This insistence on the uncompromising character of the poverty required for the kingdom of heaven and of Christian mortification is paralleled by another little addition of Luke to Mark's text: 'If any man has a mind to come my way, let him renounce self, and take up his cross, and follow me' which Luke adapts to 'take up his cross *daily*, and follow me' (Mk. 8:34; Lk. 9:23). This may be linked again with another saying of Jesus recorded by Luke: 'Keep watch, then, praying at all times' (21:36). For Luke the Christian life means total renunciation, daily mortification, uninterrupted prayer.

In the beatitudes Luke contrasts present poverty and present sorrow with riches and joy in the kingdom of God. His pre-occupation is with the individual fate of souls beyond the grave, individual eschatology.[2] 'Blessed are you who are

1 Mk. 10:21; Lk. 18:22. In Mgr Knox's version this Lucan nuance is not apparent as he has added 'all' to the Markan text as well.

2 For this see Dom Dupont's remarks, op. cit., pp. 210–13.

hungry now; blessed are you who weep now; woe upon you who laugh now.' These 'nows' are additions of St Luke, and they bring out his way of seeing the beatitudes. Whereas in their primitive meaning the contrast in the beatitudes lay rather between the condition of the world and the new messianic age already inaugurated by Jesus, the contrast for St Luke is between earth and heaven. In the original sense the poor are already in process of receiving the blessing, for Jesus is among them; in Luke's sense the blessing is still to come—reward after death, the reward of Lazarus. These senses are not in the least contradictory, one is rather the follow-through of the other; but their stress is different. Luke's interest in individual eschatology, individual salvation or damnation, is unique among the synoptics; but it is very important for his own thought. Though the great themes of classical eschatology are to be found in the third gospel, yet the second coming of Jesus appears there as something more distant, less imminent than it seemed earlier on. It would happen at the end of time but not yet, and it plays a far less dominant role in Luke's thought as a whole. Thus it has been suggested[1] that St Luke does not consider the salvific aspect of the second coming; he leaves out the Markan reference to the gathering together of the elect. The second coming is for Luke the end of the world, of sufferings and persecution, and the manifestation of Jesus' glory, but it is not the effective moment of man's salvation. Whereas Mark thinks of salvation in collective terms as linked with the glorious Parousia, Luke thinks of it individually, the fate of each man following death. Salvation will come to the elect, as it came to Stephen who 'fell asleep in the Lord' (Acts 7:59), while

[1] by Mr Jones, 'The Epistle to the Hebrews and the Lucan Writings', p. 137–8, in *Studies in the Gospels*.

condemnation will come to those who reject Jesus, as it came to Judas who went 'to the place which belonged to him' (Acts 1:25). Individual beatitude consequent upon death is the promise of Jesus' preaching and the term of the Christian life, as they are described by Luke in gospel and Acts.

The chief characteristics of that Christian life we have now seen: it was life founded upon faith in the name of Jesus and guided by the Holy Spirit; a life of poverty, prayer, mortification and persecution, of simple joy and generous sharing[1]; it was life within the community of the Church and under the guidance of its leaders, entered into by baptism and centred upon the Eucharist; and because the Church was the sole ark and means of salvation, the universal witness, it was essentially missionary and apostolic; in the period intervening before Jesus' glorious return on the clouds of heaven it had the obligation of preaching the good news and spreading forth to the ends of the earth (Acts 1:8-11). Like Paul, the Church herself had been sent upon a mission 'afar unto the Gentiles'.

If all this new life of salvation within the Christian community derived from the events of Jesus' story on earth, it derived also and even more fundamentally from something else manifested within those events: the mercy of God. Time and again the third gospel has been called the gospel of mercy; and if for St Luke the gift of salvation is the reason for the whole drama depicted in his two works, the reason for the

---

[1] It seems to me that the spirit of Christianity in St Luke's writings is very similar to that stressed by St Francis of Assisi and the Franciscan school generally. The same delight in the more human and tender aspects of Christian doctrine is linked in both with a particularly austere and exacting morality. In both Lucan and Franciscan spirituality there is a predominant concern with joy and peace as found in the practice of poverty and the acceptance of persecution.

gift of salvation itself is this loving mercy of God. 'Such is the merciful kindness of our God' (Lk. 1:78) is the constant message he is proclaiming: 'He has mercy upon those who fear him, from generation to generation' (Lk. 1:50). It is mercy which Jesus has come to teach men, 'Be merciful, then, as your Father is merciful' (Lk. 6:36)[1]; it is the meaning of the parable of the good Samaritan with its conclusion: 'Which of these, thinkest thou, proved himself a neighbour to the man who had fallen in with robbers? And he said, He that shewed mercy on him. Then Jesus said, Go thy way, and do thou likewise' (Lk. 10:36–7). If Christians must be merciful, it is in order to imitate their master and their Father. The third gospel delights to show Jesus manifesting his mercy to sinners, living with sinners and teaching to others the way of mercy and compassion, the way of the good Samaritan. He has come to earth in search of sinners like the shepherd of the parable.

If any of you owns a hundred sheep, and has lost one of them, does he not leave the other ninety-nine in the wilderness, and go after the one which is lost until he finds it? And when he does find it, he sets it on his shoulders, rejoicing, and so goes home, and calls his friends and his neighbours together; Rejoice with me, he says to them, I have found my sheep that was lost. So it is, I tell you, in heaven; there will be more rejoicing over one sinner who repents, than over ninety-nine souls that are justified, and have no need of repentance (Lk. 15:4–7).

The same parable is told in Matthew 18:12–14, but without the mention of the heavenly rejoicing over the one sinner's repentance, and without, too, that touching detail that 'he sets it on his shoulders and so goes home'. In Luke this parable is followed by the similar one of the groats, which is not found

[1] Luke's version of the Matthaean (and probably original) 'Be perfect, as your heavenly Father is perfect' (Mt. 5 : 48).

elsewhere. In his gospel Jesus is shown with especial emphasis as the searcher out of the lost sheep and lost groats, of publicans and sinners and Samaritans, dear Zacchaeus of Jericho, for example, who gladly made him welcome in his house.

> When they saw it, all took it amiss; he has gone in to lodge, they said, with one who is a sinner. But Zacchaeus stood upright and said to the Lord, Here and now, Lord, I give half of what I have to the poor; and if I have wronged anyone in any way, I make restitution of it fourfold. Jesus turned to him and said, Today, salvation has been brought to this house; he too is a son of Abraham. That is what the Son of Man has come for, to search out and to save what was lost (Lk. 19:7–10).

Right to the end of his life it is the mercy of Jesus which appears most strikingly in our gospel with two of those sayings from the cross which Luke alone records, 'Father, forgive them; they do not know what it is they are doing' (Lk. 23:34), and then to the repentant thief, just another sinner like those he had sought all through his ministry, 'I promise thee, this day thou shalt be with me in Paradise' (Lk. 23:43).

'Father, forgive them', 'As your Father is merciful'—behind the mercy of the Son is that of the Father. The mercy of God comes from the Father, but is expressed in the life of the Son, for 'My Father has entrusted everything into my hands' (Lk. 10:22). Of the Father's mercy too there is a parable, perhaps the loveliest of all, the parable of the prodigal son. In this parable the merciful heart of the Father is for ever revealed. The younger son, his money spent, his heritage wasted, repented of his fault

> And he arose, and went on his way to his father. But while he was still a long way off, his father saw him, and took pity on him; running up, he threw his arms round his neck and kissed him.

And when the son said, Father, I have sinned against heaven and before thee; I am not worthy, now, to be called thy son, the father gave orders to his servants, Bring out the best robe, and clothe him in it; put a ring on his hand, and shoes on his feet. Then bring out the calf that has been fattened, and kill it; let us eat, and make merry; for my son here was dead, and has come to life again, was lost, and is found (Lk. 15:20–4).

The theme of the sinner, of the outcast who has been mercifully found and brought into the communion of the kingdom is, in the last analysis, the central idea of the third gospel and the Acts. There is a chorus of joy, first in heaven, and then also on earth: 'Rejoice with me, I have found my sheep that was lost; Rejoice with me, I have found the silver piece which I lost; for this merry-making and rejoicing there was good reason; thy brother here was dead, and has come to life again; was lost, and is found; that is what the Son of Man has come for, to search out and save what was lost.' Rejoice because the merciful kindness of the Father has sent the Son to die for us and the Holy Spirit into our hearts for repentance and the forgiveness of sins. This is the thread which runs through the whole texture of Luke's work and makes sense of it all; it is the reason for his writing and for the truthfulness of his authorities; it is the reason of Jesus' anointing with the Spirit and his prophetical messiahship, for his journey to Jerusalem, his Passion, death and Resurrection, for the Pentecostal descent of the Spirit and the growth of the Church, for Paul's mission 'afar unto the Gentiles', for the glorification of Jesus from Transfiguration to second coming —the end, purpose and meaning of it all is no other than this, that in Jesus Christ salvation has been offered to all men and to all peoples by the loving mercy of their God.

THE HOLY CITY

WHY was St Luke so concerned with the guilt of Jerusalem? The first reason is that Jerusalem represented the old, exclusive Israel, and if there was one aspect of Christianity which especially appealed to Luke, it was its universality, its apostolate to all the Gentiles. His stress on the historical drama of the rejection of Jesus and Paul in Jerusalem was intended to bring home this underlying theological truth. Furthermore, he was living amidst the controversies stirred up by the Judaizers and the prolonged crisis provoked by the growing split between the Christian Church and official Jewry. Luke is pointing out that the responsibility for this schism lies not with the Christian leaders but uniquely with the Jews. It is they who have consistently rejected the messengers of God, be they prophets, apostles or the Son of God himself, and hence it is not surprising if they now find themselves cut off from the new church and Holy People of God.

The real problem, however, was not to convict the Jewish non-Christian body of infidelity, but to convince the Jewish Christians of the decisiveness of the schism. Loyalty to Jesus required a departure from their old ways, and Luke wished to wean them from their psychological centredness on the earthly Jerusalem. Just how much Jerusalem meant for a pious Jew of that period it is difficult for us to imagine. Jerusalem was for him truly the centre of the world, as Mount Garizim was the world-centre for a Samaritan.[1] It was where earth and heaven met, where Adam had been created, and where alone acceptable sacrifice could be offered to God. It was truly the holy city of God, the one place where God really dwelt with his chosen people, the centre of pilgrimage, the point to which one must direct one's prayers. All the deep religious sentiments of Jews for Jerusalem can be felt if one turns to read those psalms which speak of Sion, such as 124, 146, 147 and 121. Listen to the last of these:

> Welcome sound, when I heard them saying, We will go into the Lord's house! Within thy courts, Jerusalem, our feet stand at last; Jerusalem, built as a city should be built that is one in fellowship. There the tribes meet, the Lord's own tribes, to give praise, as Israel is ever bound, to the Lord's name; there the thrones are set for judgement, thrones of authority over the house of David. Pray for all that brings Jerusalem peace! May all who love thee dwell at ease! Let there be peace within thy ramparts, ease in thy strongholds! For love of thy brethren and my familiar friends, peace is still my prayer for thee; remembering the house of the Lord our God, I long for thy happiness.

This intense love and devotion to Jerusalem and the temple was increased rather than diminished by the exile and the Dispersion. Parthians and Medes and Elamites, in Mesopotamia and Cappadocia, Pontus and Asia, Phrygia and Pamphylia, Egypt and Libya, Rome and Crete and Arabia, wherever they had settled, their hearts remained in Jerusalem, and there they streamed back on pilgrimage for the great feasts to renew their devotion in the courts of the temple. Of all songs of exile the most touching was written by Jews and of Jerusalem:

[1] For the notion of the world-centre, see M. Eliade, *A Study of the Symbolism of the Centre*, Selection II (Sheed & Ward), pp. 17–43.

12

We sat down by the streams of Babylon and wept there, remembering Sion. Willow-trees grow there, and on these we hung up our harps when the men who took us prisoner cried out for a song. We must make sport for our enemies; A stave, there, from the music they sing at Sion! What, should we sing the Lord's song in a strange land? Jerusalem, if I forget thee, perish the skill of my right hand! Let my tongue stick fast to the roof of my mouth if I cease to remember thee, if I find in aught but Jerusalem the fountain-head of my content (Ps. 136:1–6).

That was how the Jew felt about the earthly Jerusalem, yearning for it with what was often, as in this psalm, far too human and natural a longing.[1] The exile should have taught them to turn their thoughts on high, 'Trust not in lying words, saying: the temple of the Lord, the temple of the Lord, it is the temple of the Lord' (Jer. 7:4).

Through the psalms the piety of each generation of Jews for David's city was nourished, but with conversion to Christianity the old loves had to be rejected. Jerusalem could be no more the holy city, no more the centre of religious life for God's chosen people; it had become instead the perfidious and adulterous city that had rejected the Messiah for which it had waited so long. Christians at first hardly realized this and very naturally continued to frequent the temple; as a result they were little molested by the leaders of Jewry. Stephen seems to have been the first to see the incompatibility between Jesus and the temple. At once, like Jesus, he was denounced, and died Our Lord's first martyr. This event was decisive: the Church could not remain temple-centred, a sect in Israel. She was all or nothing. Peter, Paul and Luke followed where Stephen had led the way.

1 See my sister's remarks on this psalm: Cecily Hastings, *Catholic Evidence, Questions and Answers* (Sheed & Ward, 1955), pp. 112–13.

The old world-centre had been rejected and the new Church did not allow of any visible world-centre at all, neither Jerusalem nor Mount Garizim nor any Christian substitute. 'You will not go to this mountain, nor yet to Jerusalem, to worship the Father . . . the time is coming, nay, has already come, when true worshippers will worship the Father in spirit and in truth' (Jn. 4:21–3). The idea of world-centre was that of the place where earth met heaven, but now this idea is realized not in a place but in a person, the Lord Jesus, and the psychological centredness of the Christian must be on him and not on any place at all. There is a new Jerusalem not made by hands, and within it Jesus is the temple.[1]

The psychological struggle which this state of affairs produced in the souls of sincere Christians was very real and very enduring. Their whole natural and supernatural world-view had been upset, and it was inevitably a painful process for them to discover over the years all the implications of their new allegiance. The issue, both psychological and theological, remained alive long after the apostolic age, and was still a

---

[1] Apoc. 21:22. It is very interesting to note that, according to the first chapter of St Luke, Our Lady was the new ark of the covenant in the months preceding the Nativity. Luke 1 must be compared with 2 Samuel, chapter 6, and in particular

> Lk. 1:43 with 2 Sam. 6:9.
> Lk. 1:56 with 2 Sam. 6:11.
> Lk. 1:41 with 2 Sam. 6:14.

The ark of the Lord stayed three months in the house of Obed-edom the Gittite, and Mary the Mother of the Lord stayed three months in the house of Zachary and Elizabeth; David said, 'How shall the ark of the Lord come to me?' and Elizabeth said 'Whence is this to me, that the mother of my Lord should come to me?'; when the ark arrived, David danced before the Lord, and when Mary arrived John danced in the womb before Jesus. Cf. R. Laurentin, *Structure et Théologie de Luc* I–II, pp. 79–81.

source of dissension in the time of St Irenaeus[1]; it was not tackled by all in the same way, and towards it we can distinguish a number of different attitudes, some orthodox, some not.

A first series may be described as Judaistic. Their most intolerant group might have justified their position with some words of Our Lord: 'Heaven and earth must disappear sooner than one jot, one flourish disappear from the law' (Mt. 5:18). All the old obligations of the law must continue to bind on Jew and Gentile alike. 'Some believers who belonged to the party of the Pharisees came forward and declared, They must be circumcised; we must call upon them to keep the law of Moses' (Acts 15:5).

A less extreme view held that, while the Gentile converts were not obliged by the Mosaic law, all the Jews were: an impossible solution which would have brought 'the middle wall of partition' (Eph. 2:14) straight down the centre of the Church whose founder's aim had been to pull the wall down.

These two views were soon seen to be inacceptable by the

---

[1] Erik Peterson has made the following interesting observations on the direction of prayer in the early Church: 'The practice of praying towards the East in the Church is in my opinion a polemical attitude countering the Jews' practice of praying towards the temple of Jerusalem. But we are not dealing with a simple opposition of fact to Judaism, but with a profound theological difference. Irenaeus (or his source), in controversy with the Ebionites, who "perseverant in his consuetudinibus, quae sunt secundum legem et Iudaico charactere vitae, uti et Hierosolymam adorent, quasi domus sit Dei" (*Adv. Haeres.*, I, 22), shows that the question of the direction of prayer was still a living problem among the Judaeo-Christians of Palestine. His conviction is that the temple is not the house of God . . . but something finished with . . . consequently we have, instead of the old direction of prayer towards the temple, the new one towards the east as the direction of Christ's return' ('La Croce e La Preghiera verso Oriente', *Ephemerides Liturgicae* (1945), p. 61).

majority of Christians, Jew and Gentile alike, and the 'Council of Jerusalem' decreed that the Gentiles at least were not to be called upon to keep the law of Moses. Little by little the extreme Judaist Christians separated from the Church and became known as Ebionites. There were many other 'judaizers' who, without going outside the limits of orthodoxy, continued to practise circumcision and the whole law, and to centre their lives on the temple of Jerusalem. They probably felt that to keep the full law was at least the way of perfection, the surest road to sanctification.

Others, outside Jerusalem, who did not practise the full law, continued to be centred psychologically on the holy city; many maintained circumcision in order to avoid persecution from their Jewish neighbours. Another important reason for keeping the law was missionary. Orthodox Jews would be so offended by the sight of a Christian Jew openly disregarding the law, that their conversion would be rendered almost impossible; for this reason St Paul circumcised Timothy (Acts 16:3). It was very difficult to know how far one should go here; it was the sort of 'adaptation' problem which Christian missionaries are always having to face. St Paul was very angry with St Peter for seeming to compromise at Antioch (Gal. 2:11–16), but others might have felt that on some occasions St Paul himself compromised beyond what was justifiable. What is important is to note that there were many questions at issue and a whole series of answers; an over-simplified division of Christians into judaizers and anti-judaizers can give a quite false picture of what was actually happening.

St Paul stood in the very middle of the battle. No one was more Jewish than he or more proud of Israel's past; no one was more concerned with the conversion of the Gentiles, or more aware that the whole economy of salvation had changed with the death of Christ: at bottom, observance of the law was a pointless thing; only faith in the Lord Jesus could justify. It was because the Jewish nation as a whole had refused this faith that they were now rejected, outside the true Israel; but this was only one act in the whole drama of salvation and must not be divorced from its context. Luke's theology of Jerusalem's rejection needs in fact to be seen within the larger whole of which St Paul spoke in chapters 9–11 of the epistle to the Romans. Here is his great conclusion:

> I must not fail, brethren, to make this revelation known to you; or else you might have too good a conceit of yourselves. Blindness has fallen upon a part of Israel, but only until the tale of the Gentile nations is complete; then the whole of Israel will find salvation, as we read in scripture, A deliverer shall come from Sion, to rid Jacob of his unfaithfulness; and this shall be the fulfilment of my covenant with them, when I take away their sins. In the preaching of the gospel, God rejects them, to make room for you; but in his elective purpose he still welcomes them, for the sake of their fathers; God does not repent of the gifts he makes, or of the calls he issues. You were once rebels, until through their rebellion you obtained pardon; they are rebels now, obtaining pardon for you, only to be pardoned in their turn. Thus God has abandoned all men to their rebellion, only to include them all in his pardon (Rom. 11:25–32).

Only once does St Luke hint at this vaster perspective of divine providence: 'Jerusalem will be trodden under the feet of the Gentiles, until the time granted to the Gentile nations has run out' (Lk. 21:24). For the rest, he is concerned with the one point of most immediate relevance, 'through their rebellion you obtained pardon'. Speaking of the various solutions to the problem of Jewish-Christian relations, Mgr Cerfaux has remarked that 'one very simple formula declares that the people of God, which in the course of its history has always been unfaithful to its mission, places today the seal on its incredulity and is definitely rejected and condemned. It is Stephen's formula. It is not Paul's.'[1] Slightly modified it could pass for Luke's. He was as fascinated as Paul by the mystery of Jerusalem and Israel—'the visible presence, and the covenant, and the giving of the law, and the Temple worship' (Rom. 9:4)—otherwise he would never have given us his first gospel chapters. But I doubt if he could also have written like Paul of 'the great sorrow, the continual anguish I feel in my heart' (Rom. 9:2) for the separation of the visible Israel from Christ.

For St Luke the essential facts were very simple, and it was of the utmost importance that every Christian should understand them aright. Jerusalem had rejected Our Lord, cornerstone of the new salvation. Therefore Jerusalem had been in its turn rejected and was no longer the centre of God's Church, which had turned instead to the conversion of the Gentiles.

Jerusalem was rejected, but not the Old Testament. Here lay the danger: to react against the judaizers to the point of abandoning the Church's whole Old Testament heritage. The author of the *Letter of Barnabas*, an anonymous little work written in Alexandria in the early second century, went far beyond holding that the temple was now a dead, rejected thing. For him it had never been pleasing to God at all, and therefore had no more than a symbolic value. Marcion, following the

[1] Mgr Cerfaux, *La Théologie de l'Eglise suivant saint Paul* (Cerf, 1948), p. 55.

same road beyond the frontiers of the Great Church, developed a radical exegetical dualism which rejected the whole Old Testament dispensation. Consequently the great war of orthodoxy in the century following St Luke was two-fronted, with Ebionites to the 'right' and Marcionites to the 'left'; in this battle St Irenaeus was the greatest of orthodoxy's champions, fighting both against a continued temple centredness and against the rejection of the whole Old Testament: the Christian Church was the fulfilment of the Old Israel, but not its prolongation.

It is well to note that St Luke also stood squarely against both errors. If his chief preoccupation was to proclaim a gospel free from the shackles of the judaizers, his intensive use of the Jewish scriptures and his first gospel chapters show that he was very far from being a precursor of Marcion. However strongly he denounced Jerusalem, we know that he was only following on Our Lord's words and that Old Testament prophets like Jeremias had already spoken out just as fiercely. Far from being a rejection of the Old Testament, the denunciation of Jerusalem implied fidelity to its deepest teaching.

Victory over a Judaistic interpretation of Christianity was certainly rendered easier by the destruction of Jerusalem and the temple in A.D. 70. The importance of this event for Christian history has not always been realized; if a cause of deep sorrow for most Christians, it was also a liberation from much of Judaism's oppressive influence, and it brought to an end the importance of the Church of Jerusalem. It was theologically important as the effective realization of Jesus' prophecies, the working out of the drama of Jesus and Jerusalem to the bitter end. A question of some importance for Lucan interpretation is whether Luke-Acts was written before or after this event, whether when Luke wrote about the temple it still existed or not, whether his 'Leave Jerusalem' was addressed to his fellow Christians when the city was still the proud, turbulent capital of Judaea or when it lay in ruins and the Judaeo-Christian world was having to re-orientate itself to a profoundly altered situation. Yet it is difficult to imagine that the outlook of Paul's Gentile friend and companion was radically altered by this event, and it is wise to follow the evidence which suggests that Luke wrote before A.D. 70 and even before St Paul's martyrdom. The prophecies of Jerusalem's destruction contained in the third gospel in no way require to have been written after the event, and to deny that the general character of St Luke's writings could belong to the earlier period is to deny that Paul could have existed at all.[1] Doubtless the Fall of Jerusalem made the psychological break easier for many Christians of Jewish origin, and it may be said to have closed the first era of Church history, but it in no way altered the essential nature of the Church or the historical experiences of Our Lord and St Paul; it was from these, not from the Fall of Jerusalem, that Luke derived his theology.

Luke's 'Leave Jerusalem' expressed a common preoccupation of early Christian teachers. 'Not all those who are sprung

[1] J. M. Creed defends a late date in *The Gospel according to St Luke*, p. xxii, while the arguments for an early one are well stated by E. Jacquier, *Les Actes des Apôtres*, pp. cxiv–cxix, and also by F. C. Bruce, *The Acts of the Apostles* (1951), pp. 10–14. As to the effect of the fall of Jerusalem on the Christian Church I agree with Dom Gregory Dix in *Jew and Greek, A Study in the Primitive Church* (Dacre, 1953), especially pp. 110–11, against S. G. F. Brandon, *The Fall of Jerusalem and the Christian Church, A Study of the Effects of the Jewish Overthrow of A.D. 70 on Christianity* (S.P.C.K., 1951), conclusions, pp. 249–51. The latter vastly exaggerates the consequences of A.D. 70 for Christianity, and his treatment of the evidence is as unreliable as Dom Gregory's very different scholarship is perceptive and enlightening.

13

from Israel are truly Israelites,' wrote St Paul (Rom. 9:6); 'I saw in my vision that holy city which is the new Jerusalem,' said St John, 'being sent down by God from heaven, all clothed in readiness, like a bride who has adorned herself to meet her husband' (Apoc. 21:2). Christians belong to a new Israel, with a new covenant, a new sacrifice, a new and invisible temple; they must not for ever be looking back regretfully on the schism, but must go out cheerfully from the old Jerusalem saying, with the author of Hebrews, 'Jesus suffered beyond the city gate. Let us, too, go out to him away from the camp, bearing the ignominy he bore; we have an everlasting city, but not here; our goal is the city that is one day to be' (Heb. 13:12–14). Let us, says St Luke, go like Stephen 'out of the city' that we too may witness to Our Lord Jesus Christ (Acts 7:57).

SELECT BIBLIOGRAPHY

The following list is by no means a complete catalogue of the works referred to in the text, still less of works about St Luke. It simply comprises a number of the more useful books on the subjects of which I have been treating. Very specialized articles, however useful, have been excluded.

BÉVENOT, M. AND RUSSELL, R., 'Christianity in Apostolic Times' in *A Catholic Commentary on Holy Scripture* (Nelson, 1953), pp. 782–824.

CADBURY, H-J., *The Making of Luke-Acts* (New York, 1927).

CERFAUX, L., *La Communauté Apostolique* (Cerf, 1953).

CERFAUX, L. AND CAMBIER, J., 'Luc' in the *Dictionnaire de la Bible* (Supplément), V (1953), Col. 545–94.

CERFAUX, L. and DUPONT, J., *Les Actes des Apôtres, Bible de Jérusalem* (Cerf, 1953).

CHAPMAN, J., *Matthew, Mark and Luke* (Longmans, 1937).

CREED, J. M., *The Gospel according to St Luke* (Macmillan, 1930).

DODD, C. H., *According to the Scriptures* (Nisbet, 1953).

DUPONT, J., *Les Problèmes du Livre des Actes d'après les travaux récents* (Louvain, 1950).

DUPONT, J., *Les Béatitudes* (Louvain, 1954).

Elie le Prophète (2 vols.), *Etudes Carmélitaines* (Desclée de Brouwer, 1956).

GIBLET, J., 'Prophétisme et Attente d'un Messie-prophète dans le Judaisme', in *L'Attente du Messie* (Desclée de Brouwer, 1954), pp. 85–130.

GREEN-ARMYTAGE, A. H. N., *Portrait of St Luke* (Burns Oates, 1955).

JACQUIER, E., *Les Actes des Apôtres* (Paris, 1926).

KNOX, W., *The Acts of the Apostles* (Cambridge, 1948).

KNOX, W., *Luke and Matthew* (vol. II of *Sources of the Synoptic Gospels*) (Cambridge, 1957).

LAGRANGE, M-J., *Evangile selon Saint Luc* (Paris, 1921).

LAMPE, G. W. H., 'The Holy Spirit in the Writings of St Luke' in *Studies in the Gospels* (Blackwell, 1955).

MENOUD, P. H., 'Le plan des Actes des Apôtres', *New Testament Studies*, vol. 1, no. 1, pp. 44–51.

OSTY, E., *L'Evangile selon Saint Luc*, *Bible de Jérusalem* (Cerf, 1953).

RAMSEY, A. M., *The Glory of God and the Transfiguration of Christ* (Longmans, 1949).

SANDAY, W. (ed.), *Studies in the Synoptic Problem* (Oxford, 1911).

STONEHOUSE, N. B., *The Witness of Luke to Christ* (Tyndale Press, 1951).

VAGANAY, L., *Le Problème Synoptique* (Desclée, 1954).

WARD, M., *We Saw His Glory* (Sheed & Ward, 1956).

INDEXES

1. *Scriptural References*

(Chapter references, where no verse is mentioned, are not included.)

OLD TESTAMENT

EXODUS

NUMBERS

DEUTERONOMY

JUDGES

1 SAMUEL

SAMUEL

3 KINGS

4 KINGS

2 CHRONICLES

2. Non-Scriptural Names